MW00626207

REPAIRING OUR DIVIDED NATION

REPAIRING OUR DIVIDED NATION

How to Fix America's
Broken Government, Racial Inequity,
and Troubled Schools

DAVID A. ELLISON

Repairing Our Divided Nation:
How to Fix America's Broken Government,
Racial Inequity, and Troubled Schools

Copyright © 2021 by David A. Ellison

All rights reserved. No part of this publication may be reproduced, stored, or transmitted in any form or by any means without written permission of the publisher, except in the case of brief quotations embodied in critical articles and reviews.

This publication is designed to provide general information relative to the subject matter covered. It is sold with the understanding that the publisher is not engaged in rendering legal or other professional advice. If legal advice or other expert assistance is required, the services of a competent professional should be sought for specific services.

Published by Cedarhurst Press

Paperback: 978-1-7376823-0-1
ebook: 978-1-7376823-1-8

Printed in the United States of America

*To those eager to do what it takes
to create a world with more civility, compassion,
compromise, and common sense*

Contents

INTRODUCTION

My first book, *Politics Beyond Left and Right: A Guide for Creating a More Unified Nation*, which was written in 2016 and published in 2017, was a call for nonpartisan leadership from a federal government that is more fiscally responsible and more socially accepting – the government, I believe, our Founders envisioned, and the one we need in order to become a more unified nation. It was also a call for our elected representatives in Washington to adopt what I call a centrist approach, as Centrists like some of the ideas from the Democratic side of the aisle and some from the Republican side, and do not feel either party has a lock on all the good ideas. Unfortunately, it seems my call has fallen upon deaf ears.

First, our federal government has not become more fiscally responsible. Even before the COVID-19 pandemic, our federal government continued to run up deficits and debt despite a roaring economy. When our nation operates with an annual deficit, it means our elected representatives spend more than the revenue it brings in each year from the taxation of *We the People*, and this will continue with the current administration's plans for more stimulus and other initiatives. Our national debt has gone from $19 trillion to over $28 trillion when you include what is owed to the federal trust funds. And this debt does not include the unfunded liabilities for Social Security and Medicare that dwarf this number. This has put our nation on a dangerous path that will put our children and all future generations in financial peril – unless something is done soon – contrary to what those who support Modern Monetary Theory say.

David Walker, the former Comptroller General of the United States, says that Modern Monetary Theory is based on a new and unproven macroeconomic theory that the United States can borrow as much as it wants as long as it borrows in dollars and inflation is under control.[1] Followers of this theory believe that the United States cannot go broke because more money can just be printed. If this were the case, why would anyone buy our government bonds? I would not. Given that higher interest rates and inflation are likely in our future, I support fiscal responsibility, not Modern Monetary Theory.

Second, our nation has not become more socially accepting. Particularly concerning to me is the racial divide we are experiencing. It has been growing now for well over a decade, and racism is at the worst level I have seen since the 1960s. It is time for our nation to set a plan in motion to solve the racial divide and create the more perfect Union our Founders envisioned.

The root of the problem can be traced back to the period just following the Civil War, a time known as Reconstruction.

After much research, I am convinced that had the leaders of our country during and shortly after Reconstruction adhered to our Constitution, our nation would not have the racial divide it has today. Because the repercussions are still affecting America, I believe that not adhering to our Constitution during this critical period in U.S. history is *America's biggest mistake*.

This nonadherence set a bad precedent that gave the false impression to future leaders that it is permissible not to adhere to our Constitution when it does not meet their personal beliefs and agenda. Since our Constitution is the *supreme Law of the Land*, it is illegal not to adhere to it, and not doing so has had grave consequences, particularly for people of color.

Some people may say that the hideous institution of slavery, an extreme form of racism, is America's biggest mistake, and I can see why they would say that. Sadly, slavery had been around for thousands of years before the United States of America was formed in 1776, and as you will learn, it could not have been eliminated immediately without risking the formation of our Union. Fortunately, our Constitution was ratified in 1787, and it put slavery on a path toward extinction. Unfortunately, it was a slow path and was not eliminated until the Thirteenth Amendment to our Constitution was ratified in 1865. Racism, however, never stopped, and I believe that when our country's leaders at that time did not use the "death pill of racism" – adherence to the Constitution – it was an even bigger mistake than slavery because racism is still haunting our nation today.

Many of these so-called leaders were blinded by a misguided belief that they were superior to black people, and this superiority complex grew into hate. One evil and destructive trait led to another. Harvard professor Jill Lepore ended her book *These Truths* with the following warning to America from Reinhold

Niebuhr, who some consider the most influential American theologian of the twentieth century and was the author of the 1952 book *The Irony of American History*:[2]

> "If we should perish, the ruthlessness of the foe would be
> only the secondary cause of the disaster. The primary
> cause would be that the strength of a giant nation
> was directed by eyes too blind to see all the hazards
> of the struggle; and the blindness would be
> induced not by some accident of nature or history
> but by hatred and vainglory."

It is time for America's blinders to come off, and for all of us to admit we still have social problems centered around superiority complexes and hate that need to be addressed. More than ever, it seems that our nation is divided by ***identification*** – whether it is by race, religion, political beliefs, gender, or sexual orientation. The United States of America is better than that, and I am convinced our Founders would be very disappointed with the conflict we have within our nation today.

It is obvious that we are a nation in desperate need of more civility, compassion, compromise, and common sense, as these are the key ingredients needed to form a more perfect Union. Now is the time for all Americans to do what is necessary for the common good of society. Now is the time to finally start following the principles that were eloquently stated in our Declaration of Independence and the laws that were established in our Constitution to carry out our Declaration's principles and promises. Now is the time to repair our divided nation.

To put us on the right path, I think we should listen to the advice Rafiki gave his friends in the Disney movie *The Lion*

King. One of his nuggets of wisdom was, "It doesn't matter. It's in the past." What a great message for reminding us that for our mental health, we occasionally need to put things behind us and move on. This is true, but not when it comes to U.S. history.

Rafiki's other nugget of wisdom is the one *We the People* need to pay attention to if we are ever going to overcome our nation's biggest mistake: **"The past can hurt. But the way I see it, you can either run from it or learn from it."** Of course, Rafiki believed in learning from the past to make a better tomorrow, and this is what we Americans need to do if we are to create a society where everyone, no matter the color of their skin, can enjoy a more peaceful and prosperous life.

Unlike my first book, which dealt with possible solutions for a variety of current financial and social issues facing our nation, this one is more historical in nature because when we take the time to understand the past, we are then in a better position to improve the present and the future.

For a long time, it has been my belief that our educational system has hurt our society by not requiring students to obtain a deep understanding of our nation's Founding, the Declaration of Independence, the U.S. Constitution, and what we Americans should expect, and maybe more importantly what we should not expect, from our federal government. Our educational system has also hurt society by not covering in detail the embarrassing subjects of slavery, racism, and prejudice. I believe if it had, race relations would be much better today. When we ignore and run from the past, we do not acquire an understanding of, nor an appreciation for, those who came before us; we do not learn valuable lessons from their triumphs and their mistakes; and we do not become a more perfect Union.

After reading this book, I hope readers will have a better

understanding of our Founders' beliefs; how the Declaration of Independence and the U.S. Constitution are inseparable and still relevant today; the negative impact racism has had on society; how deviating from our Founders' wishes has hurt our country; and how some of our country's past mistakes are still negatively impacting our nation today. At the end, I hope you will be as interested as I am in creating and implementing a plan to help those who have been most impacted by our country's past mistakes, and giving them a chance at living a life with dignity: the state or quality of being worthy of honor or respect, and having self-respect.

Nitin Nohria, the former dean of the Harvard Business School, said, "The single most important form of dignity is to feel economically self-reliant."[3] If we are to create a more perfect Union, we must make sure everyone has not only an opportunity to become economically self-reliant, but also a chance. Studies have shown that although children born into a poor household have an opportunity for success, they often do not have an equal chance for success. This is because they often have more obstacles to overcome, such as:

1. Inability to get proper nourishment and healthcare.
2. Not having access to a high-quality education.
3. Living in a poor neighborhood where they are exposed to criminals, drug addicts, or kids who look down upon and threaten those who take school seriously.
4. Growing up with a parent who may have lost faith in the ability to get ahead in the world, and chooses to pass this negative attitude down to future generations. When this is the case, direction from a good role model outside the home would be invaluable to a child. This could come

from an adult relative or friend, local businessperson, a member of the clergy, or a teacher.

To clarify, when I refer to having the chance of becoming economically self-reliant, I am not referring to the creation of huge wealth, although there is nothing wrong with that. I am referring to the worthy and realistic goal of everyone having a chance to attain the career of one's desire, a chance to live in the neighborhood of one's choosing, and a chance to live in a society where one feels safe from prejudice and physical harm.

In order to give everyone a chance at becoming economically self-reliant, we as a nation need a plan to minimize the obstacles. It is time for all Americans to join together in closing our areas of division, and it must start with giving all students across the country access to a high-quality education, so they can learn what it means to be an American and develop the skills and behaviors necessary to become a productive member of society.

Sadly, there are some in society who do not want a more perfect Union. Some continually try to keep the divide going by escalating conflicts rather than trying to solve them. These people are not to be trusted, as they are attempting to stay relevant and look out for their own interests. As Kareem Abdul-Jabbar – former basketball great, history buff, education advocate, and author of several books – said in his book *Writings on the Wall*, "These conflicts are the result of fear and misunderstanding, often propagated by those looking for political or financial gain."[4]

When writing my first book, I was often asked, "What made you decide to write a book?" My answer was always: "Anger and frustration with what is happening in our society, and I want to try to make a difference." I am still angry and frustrated, and you should be, too, if you yearn for a more peaceful and prosperous nation for all. I hope this journey into America's past will light a fire in you to do your part in helping America rise to its full potential. As you begin this book, one that I hope will play a role in moving us toward a more perfect Union, please remember Abraham Lincoln's powerful words: **"A house divided against itself cannot stand."**

CHAPTER 1

Our Founding

Let's go back to our nation's beginning and take a look at our Founders – why they risked their lives to start a new country; why they created and implemented a very specific form of government; why the principles and promises they laid out in the Declaration of Independence and the laws established in the U.S. Constitution to carry out those principles and promises make these two precious documents inseparable and still relevant today; and why they dealt with the hideous institution of slavery in the manner with which they did.

Our Founders, many of whom were great students of history and philosophy, believed in what are called ***Natural Rights*** – Rights that are universal and precede anything that is a man-made law. To understand America, you must understand the principle of Natural Rights. Since *Natural* comes from the word *Nature*, which in Latin means to be born or produced, most people believe these *Rights* are God-given. However, non-believers in God also believe in the theory of Natural Rights, but do not feel they come from a religious foundation.[1] In any event, Natural Rights shaped Natural Law, which is a higher law than man-made Civil Law. "If the law of men (civil law) does not conform with the commands of nature (divine law), [the Roman philosopher] Cicero argued that by definition, the former cannot be truly considered law, as true law is right reason in harmony with nature."[2] Our Founding was based on the belief in these God-given Natural Rights, and it differentiated America from all other nations.

So, what are these Natural Rights to which everyone in the world – not just Americans – is entitled? They are found in Thomas Jefferson's words within the first half of the second paragraph in our Declaration of Independence. His words were inspired by philosopher John Locke, who argued that "All men are born equal, with a natural right to life, liberty, and property."[3] Both Locke and Jefferson studied the work of Cicero, who believed that Natural Law was global, not regional, and that to live under such law should be the Right of all people throughout the world and throughout time. Cicero referred to this as True Law and stated that "it is constant and eternal."[4] What this tells us is that Natural Law is the principle to which all nations should adhere. Below is the portion of our Declaration that lists every human's Natural Rights, and I have highlighted them for you:

"We hold these truths to be self-evident, that **all men are created equal**, that they are endowed by their Creator with **certain unalienable Rights, that among these are**

Life, Liberty and the pursuit of Happiness. –That to secure these rights, Governments are instituted among Men, deriving their just powers from the consent of the governed, – That whenever any Form of Government becomes destructive to these ends, it is the Right of the People to alter or to abolish it, and to institute new Government, laying its foundation on such principles and organizing its powers in such form, as to them shall seem most likely to effect their Safety and Happiness."

Jefferson starts off by addressing the equality of men – meaning all men and women born into this world. Being created *equal* obviously does not mean that we are all born with equal intelligence, size, strength, looks, wants, wealth, or talents. Equal also does not include equal outcomes for all. What it means is that our Natural Rights entitle us to be treated equally as humans, which according to Locke meant that people live "equal one amongst another without subordination or subjection."[5] In the Declaration, our Founders were arguing against the inequality caused by nobility. Dr. Larry Arnn, the president of Hillsdale College, states: "In their day inequality came in the form of the king, born to rule, and his nobles, born to help him."[6] Our Founders did not believe that anyone should be permitted to inherit the right to rule.

To understand *Life* and *Liberty*, it is best to go to the 1828 *American Dictionary of the English Language* by Noah Webster, the closest dictionary I could find to the time of our Founding. Life was defined as the present state of existence; the time from birth to death. Liberty was defined as freedom of restraint, in a general sense, and applicable to the body, or to the will or mind. Nothing too controversial here.

Jefferson decided to incorporate the words *the pursuit of Happiness* rather than Locke's *property*, and the following quote from the Constitutional Rights Foundation is helpful in understanding his rationale: "By 'property,' Locke meant more than land and goods that could be sold, given away, or even confiscated by the government under certain circumstances. Property also referred to ownership of one's self, which included a right to personal well-being. Jefferson, however, substituted the phrase, 'the pursuit of happiness,' which Locke and others had used to describe freedom of opportunity as well as the duty to help those in want."[7] Jefferson saw his version as more encompassing, and the rest is history.

Declaring that Americans were entitled to the Natural Rights of Equality, Life, Liberty, and the pursuit of Happiness was bold, but the next phrase in the Declaration may have been even bolder: **That to secure these rights, Governments are instituted among men, deriving their just powers from the consent of the governed**. The well-read Jefferson learned this philosophy from Locke's *Second Treatise*, where Locke stated that "the only legitimate form of government is that based on the consent of the governed."[8] In the United States of America, this means our government only gets its authority from *We the People*, and its primary purpose is to secure our Natural Rights. Kings, of course, felt threatened by this concept.

The middle of the Declaration lists all the grievances our Founders had against King George III – among these is the King's refusal to pass laws for the accommodation of large districts of people, unless those people relinquish the right to representation in the legislature. Our Founders were certainly not about to relinquish the right to be represented. The Declaration then ends with this sentence: "And for the support of this Declaration, with firm reliance on the protection of divine Providence, we mutually pledge to each other our Lives, our Fortunes and our sacred Honor." By signing the Declaration, our Founders instantly put their lives at risk, because they demanded their Natural Rights and a government that only got its power from the People – and we all should be forever grateful and indebted to their foresight and bravery.

To secure our Natural Rights, the Founders knew that some form of government was needed because as James Madison, the chief architect of the U.S. Constitution, stated in "Federalist 51": "If men were angels, no government would be necessary. If angels were to govern men, neither external nor internal controls on government would be necessary."

"Federalist 51" is one of eighty-five essays arguing for the ratification of the Constitution. Together they make up *The Federalist Papers.* Most scholars believe that to fully understand our Constitution and its *intent,* these essays – which were written by James Madison, Alexander Hamilton, and John Jay – must be studied.

Because government's power was to be derived from the governed, the government needed to be limited in scope and power, as there was no way our Founders would have ever agreed to relinquish too much of their power again – like they had to with Great Britain. Our Constitution states what each of our three branches of government may do, and by implication what they may not do. So, limited government does not mean the size of departments or the funding levels; it means that government's powers and activities must remain limited to specifically defined areas and responsibilities as defined in our Constitution.

Because the government our Founders envisioned was to be

limited in scope and power, it is obvious that although we have a Natural Right to the Pursuit of Happiness, it does not mean that one of government's responsibilities is to provide us with happiness. What government is responsible for is providing the "conditions under which happiness, as each defines it, can be pursued, as each is equipped, by nature or nurture, to do."[9]

Because of our country's size, our Founders determined that a *republic* would be our best form of government. They felt a *pure democracy* was only appropriate for a small number of citizens, and they knew our nation would become too large for a pure democracy to work effectively. According to Webster's 1828 dictionary, a republic is a form of government where the sovereign power is lodged in representatives elected by the people, and differs from a democracy, in which the people exercise the powers of sovereignty in person. Another term for a republic is a *representative democracy*.

In "Federalist 10," Madison defined a pure democracy as a "society consisting of a small number of citizens, who assemble and administer the government in person." He went on to write that "democracies have ever been spectacles of turbulence and contention; have ever been found incompatible with personal security or the rights of property; and have in general been as short in their lives as they have been violent in their deaths." Madison much preferred a republic, which he defined as a "government in which the scheme of representation takes place."

In "Federalist 39," Madison elaborated more about the definition of a republic: "A government which derives all its powers directly from the great body of the people, and is administered by persons holding their offices during pleasure for a limited period or during good behavior. It is essential to such a government that it be derived from the great body of society, not from an inconsiderable proportion or a favored class of it."

Interestingly, as you just read, Madison referenced that our representatives should hold their offices for a *limited period.* Although *limited period* was not specifically written in the original Constitution, it can reasonably be argued that it was the intent. Proof of that can be seen in the Twenty-Second Amendment that states a president can only serve two terms. I believe that if the Twenty-Second Amendment had also implemented *term limits* for senators and members of the House of Representatives, we would have a more perfect Union today.

Notice that Madison and the Founders believed that government derived its power from the *great body of society*, not from a small, favored class. Unfortunately, we seem to have gotten away from that, as it takes a tremendous amount of money to get elected today. It is obviously time for campaign finance reform.

Oddly, there are some people who believe the Declaration of Independence and the U.S. Constitution are not connected. This is strange to me given that Thomas Jefferson, the primary author of the Declaration, and James Madison, the primary author of the Constitution, were close friends and political allies. And both individuals assisted George Mason in writing the Virginia Declaration of Rights and the Virginia Constitution. In *The Founders' Key*, Dr. Larry Arnn writes: "There is significant overlap between the text of the Virginia Declaration and the Virginia Constitution, and both overlap significantly with the Declaration of Independence and the Constitution of the United States. So, if the latter two documents are 'incompatible,' the Virginia Convention instituted this incompatibility in two documents that are as close as hand and glove. And then two of the people responsible, if one counts Jefferson as a collaborator, went on to write the Declaration of Independence and the Constitution of the United States, all while remaining the closest of political friends. And they managed, somehow, to make those two documents incompatible as well? Modern scholars ask us to believe this."[10] Note the sarcasm.

I see America as a country built upon the principles and promises of the Declaration, and implemented with the laws established in the Constitution, now the longest surviving constitution in history. And I agree with Dr. Arnn's statement that "The Founders understood the documents to be connected, to supply together the principles and the details of government, to be a persuasive and durable unity."[11]

Abraham Lincoln also saw a deep connection between the Declaration and the Constitution. He is known to have referred to our two most important documents as "an apple of gold, [the Declaration], in a frame of silver, [the Constitution]."[12] I choose to stand with Mr. Lincoln rather than with the so-called scholars of today who claim there is no connection.

There are other people who believe that the Declaration and the Constitution are no longer relevant. Think of it this way: If the Declaration does not fit today's world, that means neither do our Natural Rights. Are you willing to give up those to a more powerful government? If our Constitution no longer fits in today's world, why are our elected representatives made to take an oath to preserve, protect, and defend it? And why have there been so few amendments made to our Constitution that is 234 years old?

Kareem Abdul-Jabbar says that the U.S. Constitution is the document that defines who we are as Americans and what we stand for. He refers to it as the *rule book* for being an American.[13]

I agree with him, and I believe that all students should come out of high school with a high level of understanding of this precious document, and an understanding of the role each of us must play in society.

Our Founders were a brilliant group, but they were not perfect. They said that all men are created equal, yet many owned slaves and women were not allowed to vote. That certainly does not sound like they believed every human is born equal to all other humans. However, they declared that they did believe this in the Declaration of Independence. Unfortunately, they knew that much of our nation at that time was not ready to face the truth that all people are created equal, so what the Declaration did was give us the principles to which our nation should aspire and hopefully achieve.

The Founders, as Abdul-Jabbar stated, were creatures of their times, and that they made provisions for changing the Constitution through amendments as the country became more enlightened.[14] In this sense, the Founders did pave the way for the abolishment of slavery and the recognition of a woman's equal rights in society – two things they could not have fully implemented in 1787 without risking the formation of our Union.

Slavery had been around since the beginning of time, so it was not going to be stopped without time and effort, and it ended up causing the Civil War. As John Jay, the first Chief Justice of the Supreme Court and an abolitionist, said, "The great body of our people had been so long accustomed to the practice and conveniences of having slaves, that very few among them even doubted the propriety and rectitude of it. Then liberal and conscientious men began to draw the lawfulness of slavery into question. Their doctrines prevailed by almost insensible degrees.... We have good reason to hope and believe that if the natural operations of truth are constantly watched and assisted, but not forced and precipitated, then abolition can be achieved. Many of the legislatures in different states are proprietors of slaves, and therefore a total and sudden stop to this species of oppression is not to be expected."[15]

It is obvious within the Northwest Ordinance of 1787 – the laws for the western expansion of the United States – that the majority of our Founders were opposed to slavery and wanted to put it on a path to extinction. The Ordinance declared: "There shall be neither slavery nor involuntary servitude in the said territory, otherwise than in the punishment of crimes, whereof the party shall have been duly convicted."[16]

Even Alexander Stephens, the former congressman from Georgia, vice president of the Confederate government, and believer in white supremacy, knew our Founders did not believe that slavery conformed with the Laws of Nature: "The prevailing ideas entertained by [Jefferson] and most of the leading statesmen at the time of the formation of the old constitution, were that the enslavement of the African was in violation of the laws of nature; that it was wrong in *principle*, socially, morally, and politically. It was an evil they knew not well how to deal with, but the general opinion of the men of that day was that, somehow or other in the order of Providence, the institution would be evanescent and pass away. This idea, though not incorporated in the constitution, was the prevailing idea at that time."[17]

Abraham Lincoln understood that the Framers of the Constitution had to initially allow slavery. He stated: "They did not mean to assert the obvious untruth, that all were then actually enjoying that equality, nor yet, that they were about to confer it immediately upon them. In fact they had no power to confer such a boon. They meant simply to declare the *right*, so that the *enforcement* of it might follow as fast as circumstances should permit. They meant to set up a standard maxim for free society, which should be familiar to all, and revered by all; constantly looked to, constantly labored for, and even though never perfectly attained, constantly approximated, and thereby constantly spreading and deepening its influence, and augmenting the happiness and value of life to all people of all colors everywhere."[18]

Journalist and historian George Will wrote the following in his book *The Conservative Sensibility*: "Had the Constitution's Framers not accommodated the existence of slavery, the document would not have been written, and the nation would have been stillborn.... Had Lincoln not been willing to accept the continuation of slavery where it was – while attempting to confine it there, and thereby put it 'in the course of ultimate extinction' – he could not have won the presidential office from which he steered the nation through the war that saved the Union."[19]

Lincoln sometimes gets criticized for sounding like he was not a big believer in whites and blacks living together nor giving blacks the right to vote. I think that is unfair considering he was trying to abolish slavery, limit *States' Rights* by strengthening the federal government, and preserve the Union – and the only way to do that was to get the majority of voters to vote for him. It was a daunting task, and I assume that just like today's politicians, he would say almost anything to get elected. Harry Jaffa, a philosopher, historian, and student of Lincoln's statesmanship, stated: "If [the Founders] had attempted to secure *all* the rights of *all* the men they would have ended in *no* rights secured for *any* men.... Negroes have voting rights and serve on juries today owing in large measure to the fact that Lincoln in the 1850s disavowed any intention to make them voters or jurors."[20] Blacks have every right to be angry about the treatment their ancestors received over much of our nation's history from not only slaveholders, but also from many political leaders and judges who did not come to their rescue. However, their anger should not be directed at Lincoln.

Our Founders went to war to secure our Natural Rights, and although not all could immediately benefit from them, the Framers of our Constitution set us on a path so that once our country became, as Abdul-Jabbar said, "enlightened," amendments could be added to make it more just. So, why did we not become a more perfect Union after the Thirteenth Amendment – the one that abolished slavery, was passed by Congress prior to Lincoln's death, and ratified on December 6, 1865? The answer is *racism*.

CHAPTER 2

Racism

I believe that nearly 100 percent of Americans today acknowledge that slavery was evil. What many Americans do not know is that had the period right after the Civil War – known as Reconstruction – not been filled with racism, we all would have benefited and be living more peacefully and prosperously today – yes, even whites. Given that we cannot change history, the next best thing to do is to take the time to understand our past, learn from it, and do what can be done to shape a better future.

Racism is the lasting legacy of slavery. However, I do not believe that racism is something anyone is born with. To prove that, just go to any daycare facility and watch the young kids play. They don't care about color; they are just out for a good time with whomever strikes their fancy. Kids are wonderful that way and should be looked upon as experts in race relations. Racism is a learned behavior taught and propagated by adults – both white and black.

White people, it is important to understand how blacks were treated after slavery ended, what they had to endure, and how some Americans today are still affected by the treatment their ancestors received. I believe that improving your understanding will make you a more empathetic and compassionate person. Imagine if you were set free from slavery but were given nothing with which to start a life on your own. No land or house. No source of income. No public education for your children. No rights as a citizen. And many, maybe most, white people not liking or trusting you. Those were big obstacles to overcome, but amazingly many blacks did, and they should be honored. However, many blacks could not overcome the obstacles, and because of that, many of their descendants are suffering today. These people, as well as all people living in poor and dangerous neighborhoods, are in need of our nation's help.

Black people, it is important to understand that not all whites were racists when slavery ended, nor were they over the years that followed, and many worked to make life better for your ancestors, sometimes risking their own life to do so. It is also important to understand that just because someone does not support the Black Lives Matter organization, it does not mean they do not support black lives. I believe the vast majority of citizens in the United States today are well intentioned and are not racist. Yes, we still have too many racists – any number is too many – and it is despicable that some have been able to infiltrate the law enforcement profession. It is time for our nation to finally take action.

Racism is such an important subject that it needs to be

properly taught and discussed in our schools so the images of the atrocities that happened to blacks and others in the world are burned so deep into the minds of our youth that they gain compassion for others, that they never forget the wrongs that were done, and that they fight to never let them happen again. I am confident that by studying the history of racism, our youth will be able to lead us in the creation of a better society for all. In fact, I advocate that the History of Racism should be taught in every school in America.

When I say, "properly taught and discussed," I am referring to historical facts without a political spin. When facts are tainted with political ideologies, they can be dangerous and destructive. One such ideology is Critical Race Theory, which according to CNN correspondent Faith Karimi, is based on the premise that systemic racism is part of American society, that racism is an everyday experience for most people of color, that a large part of society has no interest in doing away with racism because it benefits white elites, that American institutions are racist, and that people are privileged or oppressed because of their race.[1] I see a lot of generalizations and inaccuracies with this "theory."

Critical Race Theory is now being taught in some universities, public schools, corporations, and government agencies, and it is not helping to repair our divided nation. Christopher Rufo from the Manhattan Institute, and many others, argues that it is based on Marxism, a system that attempts to create class conflict, eliminate capitalism, and redistribute the equity earned by others. He states: "UCLA law professor and critical race theorist Cheryl Harris has proposed suspending private property rights, seizing land and wealth and redistributing them along racial lines," and that according to Ibram Kendi, who directs the

Center for Antiracist Research at Boston University, "In order to truly be anti-racist, you also have to truly be anti-capitalist."[2] These are not the principles on which our country was founded, and they will do nothing to repair our divided nation.

As stated above, this theory has even permeated government agencies. Peter J. Wallison, a senior fellow at the American Enterprise Institute, wrote that the training materials used at the Treasury Department stated the following: "Virtually all White people, regardless of how 'woke' they are, contribute to racism," and that it "instructed small group leaders to encourage employees to avoid 'narratives' that Americans should 'be more color-blind' or 'let people's skills and personalities be what differentiates them.'"[3] In his article, Wallison also reviewed a lawsuit that was filed in Nevada on December 20, 2020, by Gabrielle Clark, the mother of William Clark, a twelfth-grade student.

William objected to what was being taught in a recently revised civics course, one that broadly classified specific racial (e.g., white) and religious identities as inherently oppressive. Students who fell into these categories, including William, were told to accept the label "oppressor." William fell into the "oppressor" category because, although his mother is black, his deceased father was white and William's skin color is light enough to be considered white. William rightfully refused to comply with categorizing himself as an oppressor and told the school that he did not want to finish the course. The school told him that if he did not do his assignments, he would fail the course and not graduate because successful completion of the course is a school requirement. No student should have to go through such an ordeal. The color of one's skin has nothing to do with the moral makeup of an individual. Education needs to be about facts, not the preaching of political ideologies.

This chapter is a brief summary of our racist past. It is not meant to shame white people. It is not meant to shame black people. It is only meant to bring an awareness to all people, in the hope that we can learn from our past so we can create a better tomorrow.

When the Civil War ended and the Thirteenth Amendment declared that slavery was illegal, it did not mean that all whites were going to suddenly stop thinking of themselves as superior to blacks. People do not suddenly change their way of thinking just because of a new law, and because of that there was still a lot of work that needed to be done in order to create a more perfect Union.

The Fourteenth and the Fifteenth Amendments were also added to the Constitution during the Reconstruction Era (1865-1877). The Fourteenth defined citizenship and guaranteed that all people shall not be denied life, liberty, or property without due process of law, nor be denied equal protection of the laws. The Fifteenth gave black men the right to vote. However, it did not give women the right to vote, something for which Susan B. Anthony and Elizabeth Cady Stanton, two of the early leaders of the Women's Suffrage Movement, had fought so hard. These women also fought for blacks to have the right to vote.

Many people forget that women in the 1800s did not have the rights they have today. It was such a bad time for women, that in 1859 Ms. Stanton wrote the following to Ms. Anthony: "When I pass the gate of the celestials and good Peter asks me where I wish to sit, I will say, 'Anywhere so that I am neither a negro nor a woman. Confer on me, great angel, the glory of White manhood, so that henceforth I may feel unlimited freedom.'"[4]

What makes the three amendments added during Reconstruction unique is that it was the first time *civil rights* were made part of the Constitution and that the federal government – not individual states – was given the power to enforce them. This was a big deal, as it took power away from the states, and many people did not like that – particularly white supremacists, many of whom lived in the South, and some who sat on the U.S. Supreme Court. Prior to the Fourteenth Amendment, states had the power to do mostly as they wished regarding civil rights, because the Tenth Amendment states: "The Powers not delegated to the United States by the Constitution, nor prohibited by it to the States, are reserved to the States respectively, or to the people."

Reconstruction is sometimes referred to as our nation's *Second Founding*. Charles Schurz, a political leader at the time, referred to this period as a "constitutional revolution [that] found the rights of individuals at the mercy of the states...and placed them under the shield of national protection."[5] In my opinion, states should have never been allowed control over the treatment, safety, and civil rights of *We the People*. We are one nation that was founded under the principle that all people are created equal, and therefore everyone needs to be treated equally. For this to happen, our federal government, not individual state governments, needs to oversee the protection of all our rights – natural, civil, and political.

When Lincoln was president, Congress established the Freedman's Bureau to help transition blacks from life as a slave to life as a free person. One of the responsibilities of the Freedmen's Bureau was to divide abandoned land in the South into forty-acre parcels and lease them to former slaves so they could work the land in order to have an avenue to self-reliance and economic freedom. Another responsibility was to help former slaves start schools for their children. Unfortunately, after

Lincoln's death, Andrew Johnson became president. He gave the land back to the plantation owners, did little to protect former slaves, and did not help them fit into society with a plan for education, job training, and citizenship.[6]

Because Johnson was a racist, it was easy for Southern states to implement *Black Codes* – a number of local laws "limiting [blacks from] freedom of movement and barring them from following certain occupations, owning firearms, serving on juries, testifying in cases involving whites, or voting."[7] Johnson had the opportunity to do something great, but he caved to the old leaders of the racist Confederacy.

State governments, particularly in the South, wanted to see blacks work, but they only wanted blacks to work for whites. Sadly, our federal government did little, if anything, to prevent this from becoming a reality. In his book *The Second Founding*, Professor Eric Foner of Columbia University states that there were Black Code laws that "required all black men at the beginning of each year to sign a labor contract to work for a white employer or face prosecution for vagrancy or other vaguely defined crimes."[8] According to Professor Carol Anderson of Emory University and the author of *White Rage*, one Philadelphia newspaper tried to explain this away, writing that the Southern states were just trying to end idleness and pauperism, and that the common belief of the time was that this would prevent former slaves from becoming a burden to society.[9] Anderson correctly points out that black people's willingness to work had never been the problem, and that having to work for free under grueling conditions with the threat of being whipped was the real issue. She states that by being forced to live under Black Code laws, "Blacks were denied access to land, banned from hunting and fishing, and forbidden to work independently using skills honed and developed while enslaved, such as blacksmithing."[10]

Freed slaves being left to start a new life with no land, no home, no food, and no money proved that the racists in our society had more control than the people who believed that all men are created equal. It is obvious that the racists wanted to keep blacks oppressed, and that they were certainly not concerned about blacks becoming a burden to society. Racists never had any real desire to have blacks become self-reliant and enjoy economic freedom. They wanted free labor from blacks and believed that whites were superior. If our government's leaders wanted the blacks to succeed, they would not have freed the slaves and then let them fend for themselves without government assistance.

Southern states did not just want free labor from blacks; they wanted to make sure blacks did not get the chance to vote and were not happy when the Fifteenth Amendment passed. Although the color of one's skin was no longer an obstacle to legally vote, that did not mean blacks could automatically vote. States have always been allowed to establish their own voting regulations and procedures, so even though it was now legal for blacks to vote, many states decided to add conditions in determining who could and who could not, with many of these conditions being too big of an obstacle for many blacks to over-come, such as ownership of property, money to pay poll taxes, and literacy tests.

Henry Wilson, a senator from Massachusetts and vice president under Ulysses S. Grant, foresaw this being a problem prior to the ratification of the Fifteenth Amendment, so he came up with his own version, which "barred discrimination in voting rights based on race, color, place of birth, property, education, or religious creed."[11] Interestingly, the Senate approved Wilson's version, but the House of Representatives did not. Wilson's version of the Fifteenth Amendment was far superior to the one ratified, but his would have been even better had he added "gender" so women could vote and made polling taxes illegal.

Before, during, and after Reconstruction, the vindictive state governments in the South were led by white supremacists who found more and more ways to criminalize blacks' behaviors and limit their freedoms. Given that the police and judicial systems were loaded with white racists, blacks found themselves in much more trouble with the law than whites, as Jim Crow laws promoting racial segregation picked up where Black Codes left off. The following are summaries of some U.S. Supreme Court cases that will give you an idea of what blacks had to endure, and how the judicial system failed them:

DRED SCOTT V. SANDFORD, 1857

Dred Scott, a slave, was taken by his owner into a territory where slavery was illegal. Scott believed that his residency in a free territory meant that he should be considered a free man. However, Chief Justice Roger Taney and the majority of the Supreme Court ruled that Congress had no power to regulate slavery in territories, and that people of African descent could not become citizens.[12]

This case is often referred to as the worst decision ever by the Supreme Court, as clearly the Constitution did give Congress the power to make laws governing territories. Justice Neil Gorsuch believes the *Dred Scott* decision cannot be defended because it does not adhere to the Constitution's original meaning. Gorsuch stated: "Virtually the entire anticanon of constitutional law we look back upon today with regret came about when judges chose to follow their own impulses rather than follow the Constitution's original meaning. [*Dred Scott* and other cases] depended on serious judicial invention by judges who misguidedly thought they were providing a 'good' answer to a pressing social problem of the day.... It may be tempting for a judge to do what he thinks best for society in the moment, to bend the law a little to an end he desires, to trade just a bit of judicial integrity for political expediency. After all, passing majorities will applaud judicial efforts to follow their wishes."[13] Obviously, Taney was a racist attempting to pursue not only his own agenda, but also that of his "partners in crime."

The *Dred Scott* case spurred on the movement for the passage of the Reconstruction amendments.

BLYEW V. UNITED STATES, 1872

Four members of a black family in Kentucky were murdered by two white men with axes. The case was moved from state court to federal court because in Kentucky, blacks were not allowed to testify in cases involving whites. The white men were convicted and sentenced to death. However, the case was overturned by the Supreme Court.

Justice William Strong, who wrote the majority opinion, was more concerned that taking the case out of state court was a dangerous expansion of federal power than he was in the conviction of the two murderers. Although cases affecting persons denied equality in state courts were supposed to be transferred to federal court, Strong felt the only parties affected by the case were the defendants and the government – not the black witnesses, and not the murder victims and their families. That does not make any sense to me, and it did not to Justice Joseph

Bradley either. Bradley wrote a dissent declaring that the majority view was too narrow, and that all blacks were affected because of their inability to testify, which was tantamount to disenfranchisement and being treated as a slave.[14]

SLAUGHTERHOUSE CASES, 1873

For sanitary reasons, the state of Louisiana and the city of New Orleans enacted a law to replace the many slaughterhouses in the city with one state-owned facility where all butchers were required to bring their cattle and hogs for slaughter. The *Slaughterhouse Cases* were a combination of the lawsuits brought by the butchers against the new law because they felt that "by establishing a monopoly the state had violated their right to pursue a lawful occupation, a principle of free labor guaranteed, they claimed, by the Fourteenth Amendment as one of the 'privileges or immunities' of American citizens."[15] The Supreme Court ruled the Louisiana law constitutional in a five-to-four decision.

Because all the butchers were white, one might assume that the Court's ruling would not have a negative impact on the black community. However, that would be an inaccurate assumption because it gave strength to states' rights, which in the South was very dangerous for blacks. It is for this reason the *Slaughterhouse Cases* are significant in American history.

UNITED STATES V. REESE, 1876

In Lexington, Kentucky, the registrars, Hiram Reese and Matthew Foushee, refused to allow William Garner, a black man, to vote in a municipal election because they claimed he had not paid a $1.50 tax, although Garner had attempted to pay, and the tax collector refused his payment. Garner brought suit, and this was the first court case regarding the Fifteenth Amendment. Reese and Foushee were found guilty, but won their appeal, and the case ended up at the Supreme Court.

In an eight-to-one decision, the Supreme Court, headed by Chief Justice Morrison Waite, upheld the appeal court's decision. Waite wrote that the Fifteenth Amendment did not guarantee the right to vote but "had merely prevented states from giving preference to one citizen over another on account of race, color, etc. [and that] the right to vote...comes from the states."[16]

This was a blatant attempt by a racist justice system to prevent blacks from voting. As I stated earlier, whites just came up with other obstacles to vote, besides color, that they knew would be challenging for blacks to overcome.

UNITED STATES V. CRUIKSHANK, 1876

The Fifteenth Amendment states that citizens cannot be denied the right to vote because of race, color, or previous condition of servitude, and the Enforcement Act of 1870, also known as the Civil Rights Act of 1870, empowered the president to enforce the law. However, during 1873 in Colfax, Louisiana, Southern Democrats were angered that African Americans voted in a Republican government, even though most of the elected representatives were white. There were threats to overturn the results of the election, and then violence erupted with somewhere between 105 and 280 African Americans murdered.

The killers were charged with violating the Enforcement Act of 1870, but in the 1876 trial, Chief Justice Waite ruled that the Enforcement Act violated states' rights, and that the

Fourteenth Amendment only protected citizens from violence carried out by the states, not by vigilantes or private acts of terror. Professor Anderson states: "The ruling not only let mass murderers go free; it effectively removed the ability of the federal government to rein in anti-black domestic terrorism moving forward."[17]

PLESSY V. FERGUSON, 1896

In New Orleans, Homer Plessy, a black man who looked white, was arrested for refusing to move from the white section of the train. This was a violation of the Jim Crow law in Louisiana requiring whites and blacks to sit in separate railroad cars. In a lower court decision, Judge John Ferguson ruled against Plessy, so Plessy took his case to the Supreme Court.

In a seven-to-one decision (one justice did not participate), the Supreme Court upheld the lower court's decision and ruled that the Jim Crow law did not violate the Constitution, "arguing that separate accommodations were not necessarily unequal accommodations, [and that] separation and equality were wholly separate ideas."[18] The Court ruling that racial segregation in public places was legal as long as the places were of equal quality was a travesty. There was never equal quality. It was clear that this ruling was just another way to keep blacks down and make whites feel superior. Justice John Marshall Harlan was the only one to dissent, and according to Justice Neil Gorsuch, Harlan's words are just as meaningful today: "In view of the Constitution, in the eye of the law, there is in this country no superior, dominant, ruling class of citizens. There is no caste here. Our Constitution is color-blind, and neither knows nor tolerates classes among citizens.... The humblest is the peer of the most powerful."[19]

Justice Harlan clearly demonstrated that Plessy's constitutional rights had been violated, but his racist colleagues voted against him, and another blemish was added to the Supreme Court's record.

I hope that after reading these cases you are as angry as I am that Justices like Roger Taney and Morrison Waite did not follow the Constitution and assured that our country would continue down a racist path. They have caused an unfathomable amount of damage to blacks, and America as a whole. Understanding our history is the first step needed to unify our nation, because understanding brings about empathy and compassion in people. That said, we know some will always harbor a dislike for and an unjustified superiority complex toward others of a different color. The good news is that with a better understanding of history, their children will have the knowledge to know that racist beliefs are wrong and that all people are equal.

It is important to note that one of the bright spots for blacks during the 1800s was Frederick Douglass, who escaped from slavery in 1838. "He initially condemned the Constitution, but after studying its history came to insist that it was a 'glorious liberty document' and that the Declaration of Independence was the 'ring-bolt to the chain of our nation's destiny.'"[20] Douglass was well-read and started speaking at antislavery meetings, becoming one of the best-known speakers in the country and the most famous black person in the world. Douglass was known to have spoken the truth, not afraid to confront society's wrongs, and he gave messages of hope.

In her book *These Truths*, Harvard professor Jill Lepore

quoted Frederick Douglass: "From slavery to Jim Crow, the history of the United States involves the necessity of plain speaking of wrongs and outrages endured, and of rights withheld, and withheld in flagrant contradiction to boasted American Republican liberty and civilization.... Men talk of the Negro problem. There is no Negro problem. The problem is whether the American people have loyalty enough, honor enough, patriotism enough, to live up to their own Constitution."[21] Douglass' message was timely then, and it is still timely today.

Frederick Douglass was correct in stating we need to speak about the "wrongs." If we do not clearly define the problem, we cannot fix the problem. That is the reason for this chapter. People need to know we have problems in this country that need fixing, several of which are a result of what happened during and shortly after Reconstruction.

The early 1900s were fraught with danger for blacks: thousands of lynchings and burnings, and no good-paying jobs available in the South, where 90 percent of blacks lived. This led to the *Great Migration* – a period when millions of blacks moved from the South to the North and West. Professor Lepore states: "Between 1915 and 1918, five hundred thousand African Americans left for cities like Milwaukee and Cleveland, Chicago and Los Angeles, Philadelphia and Detroit. Another 1.3 million left the South between 1920 and 1930. By the beginning of the Second World War, 47 percent of all blacks in the United States lived outside the South."[22]

Because of World War I, businesses in the North needed more laborers. Knowing that blacks in the South had limited opportunities to make a decent wage and get their children proper schooling, and knowing that black sharecroppers were being robbed by landowners, these businesses hired labor agents to find blacks looking to get out of the South and make a new start. Given that the South was built on the backs of black laborers, leaders in the South were afraid to lose their cheap labor and started levying large licensing fees on anyone recruiting blacks. Those getting caught without paying were subject to fines and jail time.

Southern blacks looking for job opportunities in the North got a lot of their information from the *Chicago Defender*, a newspaper owned by Robert Abbott, a black man from Chicago who was disgusted by the way blacks were treated in the South and was not afraid to say so. Professor Anderson states: *"The Chicago Defender's* threat to the old regime was clear. Nor did it flinch in the face of outrage that greeted its message. The *Defender* discussed not only the Klan but also the governors, legislators, government officials, and business leaders who benefitted from a system of oppression that robbed African Americans blind. At least as notably, the *Defender's* pages published one ad after the next about job opportunities in the North with wages that were unheard of to Southerners."[23]

Unfortunately, going to the North was not a panacea for Southern blacks. Through no fault of their own, they were not as well-educated as Northern blacks, and as a result they had different behaviors. This made it difficult for them to assimilate in a new area. Dr. Thomas Sowell of Stanford University and the author of *Discrimination and Disparities* writes: "Those blacks born and bred in nineteenth-century Chicago, and living as small enclaves of blacks in an overwhelmingly white population, assimilated culturally to the norms of the surrounding society, as other groups [such as Irish and Jewish immigrants] have in similar circumstances. The later massive migrations of Southern blacks to Chicago in the twentieth century created acute polarization within the black community there."[24] Dr. Sowell went on to say that the divide was so pronounced that the *Chicago Defender* and the pre-existing black communities in the North believed that the behavior of the Southern blacks would give blacks in general a bad name, and referred to them as vulgar, rowdy, unwashed, and criminal.

According to Sowell, blacks from the North "feared that the arrival of less assimilated [blacks] would provoke negative reactions in the larger society that would not only jeopardize the progress of their race, but would even threaten retrogressions, as the larger society turned against blacks in general."[25] Unfortunately, the fears materialized, and Sowell states that "some Northern communities where black children had for years been going to the same schools as white children, now began to impose racial segregation in the schools."[26] This demonstrates the need for getting a good education and developing the skills and behaviors necessary to be a productive member of society. Sadly, most Southern blacks did not have that opportunity, and the repercussions are still being felt in parts of our country today.

These quotes support my belief that in today's society, socio-economics, cultural traditions, and norms play more of a factor in prejudicial behavior than does the color of one's skin. The fact that whites and blacks got along well in the North prior to the migration of less educated people – in this case, blacks from the South – goes a long way toward proving my premise. It is my experience that if you are educated, have an engaging personality, are respectful of others, and are fun to be around, most people do not care about the color of your skin.

Racial segregation did not just happen in schools; it also happened in housing. Prior to the Great Migration, in cities such as Chicago and Detroit, whites did not have a problem with blacks living amongst them. However, when the Southern blacks came en masse, whites started to rebel. Real estate agents, insurance agents, bankers, landlords, and local law enforcement personnel worked together to keep blacks out of the better neighborhoods, thus forcing blacks to live in smaller areas that became less desirable as years progressed. Professor Anderson states that in Detroit, "schemes and machinations, such as redlining and restrictive covenants, [were used] to cordon off wide swaths of Detroit's housing stock from African Americans and carve a color line through the city."[27]

As blacks became more successful and wanted to move to better parts of the cities, a few were successful moving into white neighborhoods, but some had to face off against mobs and local homeowners' associations. Professor Anderson, in her book *White Rage*, gives two chilling examples:[28]

1. Dr. Alexander Turner, co-founder and head of surgery at Dunbar Hospital in Detroit, moved into an all-white section of the city in 1925. At gunpoint, with police watching, he was forced to sign a deed and relinquish ownership of his property, and then the police escorted him and his family to the black side of town.

2. Dr. Ossian Sweet was on staff at Dunbar Hospital. Sweet moved into arguably the nicest home in a blue-collar white neighborhood where most of the residents were not college educated. Knowing what happened to his colleague, Dr. Turner, he had his brother and some friends come over when he moved in, and because he was fearful of what might happen, he warned the police in advance that there might be some trouble. Sweet was also

prepared with guns if things got out of control. Rocks were thrown by the large white crowd that showed up, and windows were breaking all around them. It became too much and some of Sweet's friends and his brother started to shoot and killed two white men, including a neighbor who lived across the street. The police, instead of charging the mob outside Sweet's house, charged the house and arrested Sweet, his wife, and ten men who came to help. The police officer in charge stated that there was no crowd at the Sweets' house that would suggest the Sweets were in danger and claimed never to have seen rocks being thrown until after the shooting started. A reporter saw the whole episode, told his boss the facts that refuted what the police officer claimed, but the boss refused to run the factual story.

Sweet's legal team included the famous attorney Clarence Darrow, and after surviving a mistrial and second trial, Sweet was deemed innocent. But it was a costly victory. Sweet's wife and daughter contracted tuberculous while being held in a crowded, unsanitary jail and died, and because of that Sweet ended up killing himself.

As I mentioned, based on *Plessy v. Ferguson,* schools were supposed to be "separate but equal," but that never happened, and it took until 1954 with the landmark *Brown v. Board of Education* Supreme Court case to overturn the "separate but equal" farce. Future Supreme Court Justice Thurgood Marshall was the attorney for the NAACP, which represented Oliver Brown against the Topeka, Kansas Board of Education when Brown's third-grade daughter, Linda, wanted to go to the school close to her home, but the school system assigned her to a school that was an hour away. Marshall had been working on several similar types of segregation cases, so he was well-prepared for his courtroom battle.

Justice Stanley Reed asked Marshall whether segregation wasn't in the interest of law and order. Marshall explained that he didn't feel segregation was necessary as people had evolved since *Plessy*, and then he went on to say, "I know in the South, where I spent most of my time, you will see white and colored kids going down the road together to school. They separate and go to different schools, and they come out and they play together. I do not see why there would necessarily be any trouble if they went to school together."[29]

Justice Felix Frankfurter asked Marshall about his definition of "equal." Marshall's response: "Equal means getting the same thing, at the same time, and in the same place." He later presented to the Court empirical research showing the effects separate schools have on black children, concluding that to uphold *Plessy*, would be "to find that for some reason Negroes are inferior to all human beings."[30] Chief Justice Earl Warren declared in a nine-zero decision that the Court had ruled that separate educational facilities are inherently unequal, and had violated the Equal Protection Clause of the Fourteenth Amendment.

Interestingly, not only was our Constitution helpful in declaring segregation illegal, but indirectly, so was the Cold War. According to Professor Lepore, the Communists were using our country's treatment of blacks in their propaganda as a means to get other nations to question our devotion to democracy. The last thing the United States wanted was to have our reputation in the world damaged.[31]

The *Brown* case was supposed to be the springboard to bring about true citizenship and equality. Charles Johnson, the former president of Fisk University, stated: "If segregation is unconstitutional in educational institutions, it is no less unconstitutional in other aspects of our national life."[32] Unfortunately, the South argued that *Brown* violated states' rights and, because of that, was unconstitutional. Of course, the Southern states were wrong, but that did not stop them from allowing violence, continuing segregation, not properly funding the education of black children, penalizing blacks for joining the NAACP, and making it even harder for blacks to vote.

In the years following *Brown*, President Eisenhower could have been a big help to race relations, as he was a well-liked war hero with an approval rating percentage in the 60s, but for the most part he was silent on the subject. Justice William O. Douglas blamed Eisenhower for the years of violence that followed *Brown*, and argued, "If he had gone to the nation on television and radio telling people to obey the law and fall into line, the cause of desegregation would have been accelerated."[33]

Professor Anderson gives a great summary of America's education problem: "Since the days of enslavement, African Americans have fought to gain access to quality education. Education can be transformative. It reshapes the health outcomes of a people; it breaks the cycle of poverty; it improves housing conditions; it raises the standard of living. Perhaps, most meaningfully, educational attainment significantly increases voter participation. In short, education strengthens a democracy."[34]

Because the whole country did not get behind and support the Reconstruction amendments and the *Brown* decision, a large group of people across this country have been negatively impacted – financially, socially, mentally, and physically. Racism is cruel and immoral, and it has had lasting negative effects. Poor inner-city neighborhoods today are a direct result of the lack of a quality education being available to many black Americans since our Founding – because without a good education, you normally cannot get a good-paying job. Without a good-paying job, you cannot become economically self-reliant, and because of that, you do not get to choose where you live. Our country's past sins have stolen the dignity away from a great many black Americans, and this needs to end.

To put an end to racial inequality and ultimately racism, poor black communities need to be given the chance to attain financial success. According to *The Economist*, "Much of the material gulf between African-Americans and whites can be bridged with economic policies that improve opportunity. You do not need to build a state based on identity. Nor do you need tools like reparations, which come with practical difficulties and have unintended consequences. Economic policies that are race-neutral, which people qualify for because of poverty, not the color of their skin, can make a big difference. They have a chance of uniting Americans, not dividing them. If the mood now really is for change, they would be politically sellable and socially cohesive."[35] I agree with *The Economist*. Economic policies centered around those in poverty rather than the color of one's skin can unite our nation.

Those of us more financially well-off need to understand that people, both black and white, who grow up in poor neighborhoods have challenges most of us are not subject to, including environmental issues, lack of good healthcare and health insurance, limited job opportunities, few options for housing, nutritional challenges, and inferior schools. An example of an environmental issue is exposure to lead. Children living in substandard housing are more apt to be exposed to lead, and some end up with high levels of it in their blood, which according to

The Economist, "stunts intelligence and leads to greater violence in adulthood."[36]

I believe every child in America needs to have access to a high-quality education: one that demands mastery of the English language, math, the Declaration of Independence, and the U.S. Constitution; one that exposes students to science, the arts, and financial planning; one that develops the skills and behaviors necessary to be a productive member of society; one that demands that each student has a thorough understanding of our past, including slavery, racism, and prejudice, so they, as I said earlier, comprehend the negative impact it has had on society and fight to never let these atrocities happen again; one that teaches what our rights and duties are as an American citizen; and one that teaches the need for and benefits of having empathy, compassion, and tolerance for others.

I believe our educational system tries to push too many students toward a typical four-year high school and then a typical four-year college when clearly that is not where their interests lie. One of the goals of education is to learn a marketable skill so you can earn a good living and create your own economic success. Some people are more interested in and have the aptitude for working with their hands, and would benefit from learning a trade at a vocational school. These people should be encouraged to consider this alternate, worthwhile path. Tradesmen are always in demand, can earn a great living, and never have to worry about their job being outsourced to a foreign country. And with our aging population, the need for tradesmen will become even greater as many in the trades will be coming to retirement age. According to Earlbeck Gases & Technologies, more than 50 percent of all man-made products need welding, and that by 2024 the welding industry in the United States will have a shortage of approximately 400,000 workers.[37]

I believe that funds should be made available to train poor adults so they can gain a marketable skill in order to earn a good living. It is time for society to help lift these people up the food chain. It will help in creating a more peaceful and prosperous society for all of us, as they will then be contributing to our economy, supporting local businesses, and paying taxes.

And I want to reiterate my desire for all our *rights* – natural, civil, and political – to be overseen by our federal government, not state governments. We need uniform laws across the nation regarding all our *rights*; and that includes voting rights, which many state governments, as I stated earlier, have continually abused.

Before wrapping up this chapter, I want to bring to your attention that racism between blacks and whites is not the only form of racism we see in the world. Another form of racism that is equally horrific and despicable is ***Anti-Semitism***. According to Loolwa Khazzoom's January 7, 2020, article in *J. The Jewish News of Northern California*, the term *anti-Semitism* should be eliminated, and racism should be used in its place, as it better depicts the violence to which Jews have been subjected.[38]

To understand the negative impact racism toward Jews has had, I believe all students need to be required to learn about the Holocaust, because some uneducated, prejudiced adults try to deny that it ever occurred, and then poison their children with this untruth. I have been to Dachau, the first concentration camp during World War II. The experience was eerie and moving. I have also been to many museums in Germany to learn about the war. The Holocaust was real, and I could see that today's Germans are embarrassed by it. All forms of racism must be denounced and eliminated if we are to form a more perfect Union.

I encourage you to take the time to read Dr. Martin Luther King, Jr.'s "Letter from a Birmingham Jail" that he wrote to the clergy in Birmingham, Alabama in 1963 when he was imprisoned for participating in nonviolent demonstrations against segregation. Dr. King is a civil rights icon and a hero of mine because of his peaceful approach to effect positive change in society. I have included his letter at the conclusion of this book, along with the Declaration of Independence and the U.S. Constitution, because I believe it should go down in history as one of the most important pieces in American literature and be required reading in schools. I believe that children and teens who read this letter will be moved by his words and become excited about joining those of us who are seeking a more civil, compassionate, and just society. I hope Dr. King's words move you as much as they have moved me.

CHAPTER 3

Living Up to Our Constitution

Frederick Douglass challenged Americans when he questioned whether we had loyalty enough, honor enough, and patriotism enough to live up to our Constitution. In the last chapter, you saw that even the Supreme Court didn't always live up to our Constitution, as on occasion the justices would allow their personal feelings to get in the way of a constitutional decision. At the end of this chapter, I hope you will agree with me that the Supreme Court justices should never allow their personal feelings to factor into a decision, and that their job is to render legal decisions, not to create law.

The definition of our Constitution is found in Article VI of the Constitution. It states that the Constitution is the **supreme Law of the Land**. It also states that all senators, representatives, state legislatures, and all executives and judicial officers, both of the United States and of the several states, shall be bound by oath or affirmation, to support the Constitution. So why is it that some people feel they can interpret the Constitution in ways other than what the Framers intended? I believe the answer is that some people would rather promote their own agenda than follow the Law of the Land.

For example, in *Dred Scott v. Sandford*, it is obvious that when Chief Justice Taney and the majority ruled that Congress did not have the power to outlaw slavery in the territories, when in fact the Constitution gave Congress the power to make laws governing territories, they were doing it to promote their own agenda: their desire for the continuance of slavery.

It has long been my belief that the only way to interpret the Constitution correctly is by the analysis of the words used, the intent of its Framers, and how it was interpreted by the readers at the time it was written. The meaning of the Constitution never changes, unless an amendment is added. This line of thinking is called *Originalism*, and it is the thought process the judicial system should be required to use, since they are not tasked to create law.

Justice Neil Gorsuch stated in his book *A Republic, If You Can Keep It*: "For a judge bound to respect and not violate the terms of a written law he has sworn to support, the natural starting point for resolving any dispute over its meaning must be the ordinary meaning of that term at the time of its enactment. After all, that's how we interpret *every* text. When Hamlet threatens to 'make a ghost of him that *lets* me,' the reference may seem unclear to a modern reader. But when you look at a contemporaneous dictionary you quickly discover that 'let' meant 'hinder' (as the term is still used in tennis today, when the ball is hindered by the net [on a serve]). So, most everyone today would agree that Hamlet was not threatening to kill someone who *wanted* to be killed; it's clear that Hamlet was threatening to kill anyone who *got in his way.* Confusion solved by the original public meaning."[1]

There are some opponents to an Originalist interpretation of the Constitution because they believe things have a way of changing over the years, and we need more of a *Living Constitution* to keep up with the changes. On the surface it sounds reasonable, but not in its application. If our Constitution were considered a *living document,* our laws would continually be in flux, as they would be subject to the whims of the day or period of time. As you just saw, this did not play out well for blacks over the years.

Justice Gorsuch explains that although the Constitution's original meaning is fixed, new applications of the meaning will arise with new developments and new technologies. He gives some examples:[2]

1. In the Eighth Amendment's Cruel and Unusual Punishments Clause, "cruel" is referring to the infliction of pain. That never changes, but that meaning doesn't only encompass those particular forms of torture known at the Founding; it also includes more modern methods.

2. As originally understood, the First Amendment protected speech. That guarantee does not only apply to speech on street corners or in newspapers; it also applies to speech on the internet.

3. The Fourth Amendment, as originally understood, required the government to get a search warrant to search a home. Now that meaning applies whether the government seeks to conduct a search the old-fashioned way by

rummaging through a home or in a more modern way by using a thermal imaging device.

Some, including Professor Jack Balkin from the Yale Law School and George Will, refer to discerning and applying the Framers' original intent to contemporary circumstances as *Living Originalism*.[3]

Justices on the Supreme Court are appointed to interpret law, not to make it. They do not have to run for office; they are appointed. They should have no allegiance to any one person, group of people, or their own personal feelings. They should only have allegiance to the U.S. Constitution. Since 1869, there have consistently been nine justices serving on the Supreme Court at any one time. Prior to that, Congress periodically changed the number of justices to achieve its own partisan political goals. For the sake of nonpartisanship, it is in everyone's best interest to stay with nine. "Only because he understood judging to be a distinct discipline guided by neutral interpretive principles could [Alexander] Hamilton credibly argue that the judiciary would be the 'least dangerous' branch and would exercise merely 'judgement' and not 'will'.... The goal is not to 'do justice' as the judge may personally see it, but to enforce the Constitution as written."[4]

If we did not have Originalism to guide the Court in the interpretation of the Constitution, none of us would know what rights we have or when our rights are being violated. Justice Benjamin Robbins Curtis said in his dissent of the *Dred Scott* decision: "When a strict interpretation of the Constitution, according to fixed rules which govern the interpretation of laws, is abandoned, and the theoretical opinions of individuals are allowed to control its meaning, we have no longer a

Constitution; we are under the government of individual men, who for the time being have power to declare what the Constitution is, according to their own views of what it ought to mean."[5] History has shown that not adhering to the Constitution has not worked out well for *We the People*.

I do not want to live in a world where laws or interpretations of laws are constantly changing because of the beliefs and desires of people who temporarily hold elected office or hold a position to which they have been appointed. Allowing that to occur means that it could be possible for you to be arrested today for something you did in the past that was legal at the time. If you do not want that to happen to you, you are an Originalist, and Frederick Douglass would be proud of you.

Being a justice is difficult, because it sometimes requires voting not only against the majority of the public's opinion, but also against one's own personal opinions and values. We do not need justices who represent the far left or the far right. We do not need justices who represent the "issue of the day." We need justices who represent the original intent of the U.S. Constitution. Justice Gorsuch stated: "I hope you will remind those you encounter that if they want to secure their own liberty from oppression, they should want lawyers and judges who are unafraid to follow the law where it leads and enforce the law fearlessly, without bending to the passing whims and wishes of public opinion. For one day, too, you might remind your friends, they could find themselves braced against the prevailing winds of the day, in need of a lawyer and facing a judge. And when that day comes, I hope you will ask them, would they rather stand before a court of public opinion or a court of law?"[6]

Let's all demand that our elected leaders, those in our judicial system, and all Americans become *Living Originalists*, so we can form the more perfect Union most of us desire.

CHAPTER 4

Democracy:
Attributes and Threats Against

Throughout time, our republic – our representative democracy – has gone in and out of crisis because the principles and promises in our Declaration of Independence and the laws written in our Constitution have not suited the personal beliefs and prejudices of some of our elected representatives and some members of the Supreme Court. You have now seen some of these instances, and I hope you found them to be as appalling as I have.

Let's now look at what we need in order to have a well-run society. In their book *Four Threats*, Professor Suzanne Mettler of Cornell University and Professor Robert Lieberman of Johns Hopkins University list four key attributes to an effectively functioning representative democracy:[1]

1. **Free and Fair Elections**. Having the right to vote may be the most important benefit of a representative democracy. If run fairly, elections are the most civil and humane way to choose the best people for the task of leading us toward a more perfect Union. And if they do not lead us in that direction, we can vote them out of office. I believe that Election Day should be a national holiday, and I would do that by combining it with Veterans Day. It would be a great way to honor our veterans who risked their lives so we would have the right to vote.

2. **Must Adhere to the Rule of Law**. The important thing to remember is that no individual is above the law. That is why all citizens, including those in government, must follow our Constitution and our laws. Our representative democracy cannot afford to have our citizens or our elected leaders take the law into their own hands.

3. **Legitimacy of the Opposition**. We all must recognize that those with different political beliefs or party affiliations from our own are not our enemies and not necessarily a threat. They are fellow citizens with equal stakes in the contest and an equal right to participate. A representative democracy does not work when one party makes it impossible for another party to compete effectively or to govern when it wins an election.

4. **Integrity of Rights**. Government must protect the *integrity of rights*, including civil liberties, such as freedom of speech, freedom of religion, and freedom of the press; civil rights, such as ensuring that people cannot be turned away from jobs, schools, restaurants, or housing on the basis of their race, religion, or sex; and voting rights.

Unfortunately, a fully functioning representative democracy is always subject to what Mettler and Lieberman call the *four threats*:

1. **Political Polarization.** "Not many years ago, lawmakers in Washington frequently cooperated across party lines, forging both policy alliances and personal friendships. Now, hostility more often prevails, and it has been accompanied by brinkmanship and dysfunction that imperil lawmaking on major issues."[2] Political parties seem more interested in winning elections than properly governing and doing what is in the best interest of *We the People.* Sadly, things are so partisan today that some families and friends can no longer civilly discuss politics and current events, and with some it has gotten so bad that they are no longer speaking to one another. I long for the days when Ronald Reagan and Tip O'Neil would sit down, have a cocktail, and civilly discuss their differences regarding issues, and then after some compromising, work out a deal.

2. **Determining Who Belongs**. Although our Declaration of Independence states that all people are created equal, it is obvious that some have been made to feel less equal than others. "When a nation features deep social divisions along lines of race, gender, religion, or ethnic group, some citizens may favor excluding certain groups or granting them subordinate status.... [And some] politicians may deliberately seek to inflame divisions as a political strategy that can unite and mobilize groups who would not otherwise share a common goal."[3] I hope I have proven to you that this is not what our Founders wanted.

3. **Economic Inequality**. This can cause a lot of strife between society's so-called haves and have-nots. The question is, what is the best way to handle the economic gap? This subject will be addressed in Chapter 10.

4. **Executive Aggrandizement**. This occurs when presidents attempt to expand their power by taking away some of the powers of Congress. "Presidents throughout the twentieth century have expanded the powers of the office, whether through the use of executive orders and proclamations, the administrative state, an enlarged White House staff and creation of the Executive Office of the Presidency, or the presidency's control over foreign policy and national security. Meanwhile, Congress – typically in moments of crisis, whether related to foreign policy or domestic travails – has ceded considerable authority to the executive branch and enabled presidents to act unilaterally and often without oversight."[4] Congress ceding its authority and responsibility will be discussed in the next chapter.

I will add another threat to our representative democracy – the media, both mainstream and social. Today, it is so hard to determine fact from fiction because most of what we hear and read is opinion. A few years ago, I heard Leslie Stahl from *60 Minutes* speak at a breakfast meeting for the benefit of the Cardinal Shehan Center, an organization in Bridgeport, Connecticut that does some great things for the city's youth. She told the story about when she first started working in journalism, reporters were to just ask questions and listen. They were not allowed to comment, smirk, or roll their eyes. They were to leave the interpretation of the responses to the viewers and readers. We no longer see much of that.

Television and radio shows that are supposedly dedicated to the news are often platforms for spreading political ideologies (often carefully cloaked as straight news/journalism) and use sensationalism to boost ratings. Social media is often used similarly, with a lot of misinformation and vitriol being spread. I miss great journalists, such as Walter Cronkite and Tim Russert. Mr. Cronkite was considered "The Most Trusted Man in America." Mr. Russert would ask each guest tough questions on *Meet the Press*. And when they were on the air, you could never tell which side of the political aisle either of them was on.

A kinder, gentler media without an agenda other than to spread the truth, not someone's version of the truth, would help to unify our nation.

Long live our representative democracy, aka a republic!

CHAPTER 5

Congress's Dereliction of Duty

Some constitutions make promises that on the surface sound wonderful, such as free education and free healthcare. Ours is different. It is not so much about what government will do for us; it is more about what government cannot do to us. As Justice Neil Gorsuch wrote, "From their own experience and understanding of history, the framers knew that to prevent the rule of law from becoming the rule of men more is required than a Constitution full of nice promises. What's needed is a Constitution that counteracts the instinct to seek and misuse power, one that secures individual rights not so much by their enumeration as by real structural limits on the power of government and those who run it."[1]

It is clear that the Framers were specific that only those powers enumerated in the Constitution are enforceable. As such, our government was designed to be limited in scope and power. As further proof that our Framers were only giving the federal government certain, enumerated powers, one needs to read *The Federalist Papers*, as it provides insight into what they were thinking when they created the Constitution and were trying to get it ratified by the states.

From "Federalist 41," written by James Madison:

"It has been urged and echoed, that the power 'to lay and collect taxes, duties, imposts, and excises, to pay the debts and provide for the common defense and general welfare of the United States,' amounts to an unlimited commission to exercise every power which may be alleged to be necessary for the common defense or general welfare. No stronger proof could be given of the distress under which these writers labor for objections, than their stooping to such a misconstruction."

"For what purpose could the enumeration of particular powers be inserted, if these and all others were meant to be included in the preceding general power? Nothing is more natural nor common than first to use a general phrase, and then to explain and qualify it by a recital of particulars. But the idea of an enumeration of particulars which neither explain nor qualify the general meaning, and can have no other effect than to confound and mislead, is an absurdity...."

From "Federalist 45," written by James Madison:

"The powers delegated by the proposed Constitution to the federal government are few and defined. Those which are to remain in the State governments are numerous and indefinite. The former will be exercised principally on external objects, as war, peace, negotiation, and foreign commerce; with which last the power of taxation will, for the most part, be connected. The powers reserved to the several States will extend to all the objects which, in the ordinary course of affairs, concern the lives, liberties, and properties of the people."

From "Federalist 83," written by Alexander Hamilton:

"The plan of the convention declares that the power of Congress, or, in other words, of *national legislature*, shall extend to certain enumerated cases. This specification of particulars evidently excludes all pretension to a general legislative authority, because an affirmative grant of special powers would be absurd, as well as useless, if the general authority was intended."

Our Framers divided the powers of our federal government among the following three branches:

1. **Legislative**: To make the laws by which we live, within the limitations enumerated in the U.S. Constitution.
2. **Executive**: To execute the laws created by the Legislative body, and act as commander in chief of our armed services.
3. **Judicial**: To try civil and criminal cases and make judgments on the constitutionality of the laws implemented by the other branches. The Judicial branch is not to create laws.

The separation of powers among the three branches provides the checks and balances needed to assure no one branch obtains too much power, as the Framers wanted to make sure our unique form of government could stand the test of time, change, and elected officials whose leadership skills leave a lot to be desired. As James Madison wrote in "Federalist 10": "Enlightened statesmen will not always be at the helm."

What our government was not designed for is one branch ceding some of its power to either another branch or an outside agency. This is in direct violation of our Constitution and a dereliction of duty because it takes power away from *We the People*. Our power comes from being able to vote into office people we trust, and then vote them out of office when we determine there is a better option. This power is lost when elected officials abdicate their responsibilities, because then we no longer know their job description, their beliefs, or what they stand for.

The Legislative branch, not the president, was given the power to make the laws by which we live. Unfortunately, Congress has been derelict in its duty to follow Article I, Section 1, of the U.S. Constitution: "All legislative Powers herein granted shall be vested in a Congress of the United States, which shall consist of a Senate and House of Representatives." These powers are enumerated in Article I, Section 8. Nonetheless, on numerous occasions over the years, presidents have taken it upon themselves to institute what are almost as powerful as laws: *Executive Orders*. The editors of *History.com* state: "With an executive order, the president instructs the government how to work within the parameters already set by Congress and the Constitution. In effect, this allows the president to push through policy changes without going through Congress."[2] The Supreme Court can invalidate an executive order if it deems the order to be unconstitutional, and Congress can overturn an executive order by passing a new law. However, even with these checks and balances being available, it has resulted in the ever-increasing power of the president, which is not what our Framers intended.

In other instances, Congress has delegated its lawmaking power to the Executive branch and in turn unaccountable *administrative agencies*. Justice Clarence Thomas would like to see the Judicial branch limit the Legislative branch's ability to delegate its power, and states, "The Court has overseen and sanctioned the growth of an administrative system that concentrates the power to make laws and the power to enforce them in the hands of a vast and unaccountable administrative apparatus that finds no comfortable home in our constitutional structure."[3]

Over time we have seen more administrative agencies formed that end up being very powerful and unaccountable to Congress, sometimes the president, *We the People*, and even our judicial system. According to Michael Rappaport, a professor of law at the University of San Diego School of Law, "[Administrative] agencies exercise not merely the executive power of enforcing the laws, but also substantial legislative and judicial power. Congress has delegated significant authority to agencies to enact numerous regulations and to adjudicate a multitude of cases.... If agency officials are not checked, they can use that authority toward problematic objectives, such as pursuing extreme ideologies or promoting the interests of a political party, the bureaucracy, or concentrated groups."[4]

Administrative agencies include the Environmental Protection Agency, Consumer Financial Protection Bureau, Federal Trade Commission, Federal Communications Commission, Food and Drug Administration, Drug Enforcement Administration, Securities and Exchange Commission, Customs and Border Protection, Economic Development Administration,

Education Department, Transportation Department, Treasury Department, and many, many more.

These administrative agencies wield so much power that some people refer to them as the *fourth branch of government*. Let's review some examples of these agencies in action:

1. The Federal Trade Commission (FTC) is allowed to create rules of conduct, investigate potential infractions, prosecute those in violation, and then adjudicate the case. The Commission can decide whether the adjudication takes place before the full Commission or before a semi-autonomous administrative law judge. If the Commission decides on an administrative law judge, but then does not like the verdict, the Commission can appeal the decision to the Commission.[5] It sounds like the FTC can be judge, jury, and executioner.

2. The Consumer Financial Protection Bureau's budget does not come from a congressional appropriation. According to Dr. Arnn, "There is no ability in principle for elected branches [of government] to tailor its cost to overall public priorities. Instead, it gets its funds from a percentage of the revenues of the Federal Reserve, which are themselves locked in a dark box that Congress has been trying to crack open for years."[6]

3. The Environmental Protection Agency (EPA) had permission, via Congress's passage of the Clean Air Act, to put whatever limits it deemed necessary on pollutants in order to protect the public's health. The EPA decided to mandate tolls on some New York City bridges in order to raise funds to support mass transit because it believed that would lead to fewer automobiles on the road and,

therefore, a reduction in air pollution. According to George Will, "In response to angry constituents, some members of Congress representing the city – members who had voted for this capacious grant of policy-making power to the EPA – led a march to protest what they had done in delegating their policy-making responsibilities."[7] You cannot make this stuff up.

4. According to Senator Mike Lee from Utah, "a single statute empowering the Food and Drug Administration (FDA) to make rules for 'medical devices' had led to the FDA's regulation of weight-lifting equipment, mouthwash, sunglasses, and television remote controls."[8] This looks like overreach to me.

I think you get the point. These administrative agencies are making regulations that have the force of law, they can levy fines and send people to jail, and if one appeals, he or she has to go before the agency that has already convicted them. Yes, agencies are required to follow procedures and are subject to judicial review. However, according to Justice Gorsuch, because of the *Chevron* doctrine (a Supreme Court case), "If a statutory term is ambiguous, a judge must accept any reasonable gloss on the law the agency can supply – even if the judge is convinced it's not the *best* reading of the statute's terms. The related *Auer* doctrine requires judges to do much the same for an agency's interpretation of its own regulations. So now, not only do executive agencies get to write regulations, not only may they enforce them too, but they are even allowed to resolve ambiguities that later emerge in favor of their preferred policy outcomes."[9]

Justice Thomas stated: "[Courts] have deferred to an agency's interpretation of a *different* agency's regulations. They've deferred to agency interpretations that were inconsistent with the agency's previous interpretations of the *same* statute or regulation. They've deferred to agency interpretations advanced for the first time in litigation. They've deferred to agency interpretations when it comes to criminal sentencing. Under the *Brand X* doctrine, the Supreme Court has even said that courts must sometimes overrule their preexisting judicial interpretations of the law when an executive agency wants a different result."[10] Obviously, something is wrong when our judicial system shows deference to an administrative agency.

The supporters of these administrative agencies argue that big government programs require a specific level of expertise that members of Congress do not have, and that it is cost-effective. To that extent, Professor Rappaport agrees with them. However, he believes improvements need to be made to the system, and he has some ideas that seem to make sense.

To secure the benefits of expertise and cost savings, Rappaport argues: "One cannot rely on ordinary federal courts hearing all agency adjudications and Congress legislating regulations from scratch. Instead, expert and independent administrative courts should hear agency adjudications and Congress should decide whether to approve major regulations written by administrative agencies."[11] His approach would be a step in the right direction, as it would bring back the *separation of powers* that we have been missing. To accomplish this, Rappaport recommends the following:[12]

1. When one is appealing an administrative law judge's decision, it should be before an independent court – not the heads of an agency – and the judges must have expertise

in economics, medicine, or science, depending on which area of expertise the case requires.

2. Only Congress should be allowed to enact laws that have an annual cost to the economy of $100 million or more, as that would return a significant portion of administrative agencies' legislative power to Congress. The procedure would be for administrative agencies to draft the regulations and leave Congress the role of approving or disapproving them.

3. Deference to administrative agencies' interpretations of legal matters must be greatly reduced or eliminated.

Sometimes it is easier for members of Congress to shirk their responsibility to create the laws and rules we live by, particularly when dealing with controversial subjects. They can avoid taking a direct stand on an issue they feel could hurt them in the next election, yet still look good "back home" if they can report to their constituents that they created legislation to have the "experts" at an administrative agency solve the problem. And if their constituents end up not liking the agency's solution, they can just blame it on the agency. Pretty convenient, wouldn't you agree?

It is time for Congress to stop abdicating its responsibilities and start adhering to the *separation of powers* our Framers brilliantly instituted.

CHAPTER 6

The Need for Liberal Thinking

Racism is not the only cause of divide in our country today. Politics is also to blame, and we need liberal thinkers to bring us closer together. To clarify, I am not referring to a liberal thinker as being part of any specific political party; there have always been liberal thinkers on both sides of the aisle. In Noah Webster's 1828 dictionary, *liberal*, as it relates to politics, is defined as the following: Not selfish; catholic; enlarged; embracing other interests than one's own; as *liberal* sentiments or views; a *liberal* mind; *liberal* policy.

The Economist, one of the world's most respected magazines, has been in publication since 1843. Their 175th anniversary issue explained that it was created "to campaign for liberalism – not the leftish 'progressivism' of American university campuses or the rightish 'ultraliberalism' conjured up by the

French commentariat, but a universal commitment to individual dignity, open markets, limited government and a faith in human progress brought about by debate and reform."[1] Not the definition you are accustomed to, is it?

Our Founders were liberal thinkers, and they sure did have spirited debates, as each was looking to promote his interpretation of what the best path should be for a newly formed country. There are two groups of liberal thinkers, but before defining them, it might be interesting for you to answer a few questions that Yuval Levin posed in his book *The Great Debate*, since your answers will give you a better understanding of what is important to you:[2]

1. Should our society be made to answer to the demands of stark and abstract commitments to ideals like social equality or to the patterns of its own concrete political traditions and foundations?

2. Should the citizen's relationship to society be defined above all by the individual right of free choice or by a web of obligations and conventions not entirely of their own choosing?

3. Are great public problems best addressed through institutions designed to apply the explicit social knowledge of experts or by those designed to channel the implicit social knowledge of the community?

4. Should we see each of our society's failings as one large problem to be solved by comprehensive transformation or as a set of discrete imperfections to be addressed by building on what works tolerably well to address what does not?

5. In confronting the society around us, are you first grateful for what works well about it and moved to reinforce and

build upon that, or are you first outraged by what works poorly and moved to uproot and transform it?

6. Do you want to alleviate poverty through large national programs that use public dollars to supplement the incomes of the poor or through efforts to build on the social infrastructure of local civil-society institutions to help the poor build the skills and habits to rise?

According to Levin, your answers reflect your current opinion of the state of our society, your assumptions about how much knowledge and power social reformers will have on society going forward, and which way you lean politically. One group of liberal thinkers follows a politics of vigorous progress toward an ideal goal, and the other a politics focused on preservation of a precious inheritance and improving upon that which is not working well in society.[3] He calls the former *progressive liberalism* and the latter *conservative liberalism*. Both groups are well intentioned, and as Levin says, each group is "passionately advancing its understanding of the common good."[4]

Personally, I believe that society's problems are best solved by preserving that which has worked well over time (for example, a federal government with three branches in order to have a system of checks and balances), and gradually – sometimes urgently – improve that which has not. I do not believe that some sort of utopian society where people are free from material want and obligations is possible. I do believe Nitin Nohria is correct that the most important form of dignity is to feel economically self-reliant. I am a believer that our country's founding documents, the Declaration of Independence and the U.S. Constitution – both of which the original leaders of the *progressive movement* in the late 1800s and early 1900s declared to be outdated – are our guides to a more perfect Union. I guess that makes me lean more toward the *conservative liberal* camp.

Professor Ronald Pestritto of Hillsdale College has this to say about Progressivism: "In its essence it amounts to an argument in favor of progressing, or moving beyond, the political principles of the American Founding….These Progressives and their contemporaries took aim both at the Constitution, where the separation of powers inhibited the kind of activist central government that would be essential to implementing the Progressive policy agenda, and at the Declaration of Independence, which the Progressives rightly understood as setting the purpose for the Constitution itself."[5] Progressives have had a desire to expand the scope of government because they believe our Founders' government was not designed to handle the economic and social conditions of the modern era. I think I have already demonstrated that not following our Constitution does not bode well for society, so I am not in the progressive camp.

Some progressives have included presidents Theodore Roosevelt, Woodrow Wilson, and Franklin Roosevelt, and also several academics who thought they could mold future generations, including Frank Goodnow, John Dewey, and Charles Van Hise. Professor Pestritto stated that in his 1932 Commonwealth Club Address, Franklin Roosevelt, who was known to have believed the Constitution to be too inflexible, "credited the ideas of Theodore Roosevelt and especially Woodrow Wilson as the source of his own plan for transforming American government."[6]

According to Pestritto, Woodrow Wilson, our twenty-eighth president, who was known to be racist and not a believer in *natural rights*, "came to see the Constitution as a cumbersome instrument unfit for the government of a large and vibrant nation."[7] Wilson did not believe in our Constitution's *checks and balances* and the *separation of powers* and believed that Congress had too much power because that branch of our government makes the laws. He wanted the president to have the lion's share of the power. Wilson said that "We have grown more and more inclined from generation to generation to look to the President as the unifying force in our complex system, the leader both of his party and of the nation.... His office is anything he has the sagacity and force to make it."[8] My research shows that Wilson believed he could improve, if not perfect, just about anything, from people to societies. I believe he would have been more comfortable as a king than as a president.

Regarding Wilson's views on our *natural rights*, it sounds like he was claiming to be more intelligent than John Locke and Thomas Jefferson. President John F. Kennedy might take exception to this claim. At a dinner honoring a group of Nobel Prize winners in 1962, Kennedy stated: "I think this is the most extraordinary collection of talent, of human knowledge, that has ever been gathered together at the White House, with the possible exception of when Thomas Jefferson dined alone." Kennedy was certainly on Jefferson's side regarding *natural rights*, and declared, "The rights of man come not from the generosity of the state but from the hand of God." I do not think Kennedy and Wilson would have seen eye to eye.

In 1916, Frank Goodnow, the former president of Johns Hopkins University and a person who did not subscribe to the theory of *natural rights* that our Founders believed were bestowed upon us by our Creator, believed that people's rights came from the society to which we belong.[9] My question is, if our Creator, or the universal power nonbelievers in God believe in, is not determining people's rights, who is? This so-called progressive line of thinking runs counter to our Declaration of Independence.

In his 1916 speech at Brown University, Goodnow stated: "We no longer believe as we once believed that a good social organization can be secured merely through stressing our rights. The emphasis is being laid more and more on social duties. The efficiency of the social group is taking on in our eyes a greater importance than it once had. We are not, it is true, taking the view that the individual man lives for the state of which he is a member, and that state efficiency is in some mysterious way an admirable end in and of itself. But we have come to the conclusion that man under modern conditions is primarily a member of society and that only as he recognizes his duties as a member of society can he secure the greatest opportunities as an individual.... We teachers are in a measure responsible for the thoughts of the coming generation. This being the case, if under the conditions of modern life it is the social group rather than the individual which is increasing in importance, if it is true that greater emphasis should be laid on social duties and less on individual rights, it is the duty of the University to call the attention of the student to this fact and it is the duty of the student when he goes out into the world to do what in him lies to bring this truth home to his fellows."[10] I prefer to follow our Declaration and our Constitution rather those who believe these two precious documents are no longer relevant.

In 1935, Professor John Dewey from Columbia University wrote: "The only form of enduring social organization that is now possible is one in which the new forces of productivity are cooperatively controlled and used in the interest of the effective liberty and cultural development of the individuals that constitute society. Such a social order cannot be established by an unplanned and external convergence of the actions of separate individuals, each of whom is bent on personal private advantage."[11] Our Founders were not looking for a large, controlling federal government, and definitely would not trust a government that was not based on open markets and capitalism.

In his book *The Conservative Sensibility*, George Will stated: "Progressives held that by using government power to change social conditions, predetermined social ends could be attained. It was a short step from here to the project of not just reforming social conditions but directly modifying human stock."[12] One of the followers of this philosophy was Charles Van Hise, the former president of the University of Wisconsin, who argued: "We know enough about eugenics so that if that knowledge were applied, the defective classes would disappear within a generation."[13] Eugenics is the science of improving a human population by controlled breeding to increase the occurrence of desirable heritable characteristics, and that sounds a little too much like the beliefs of Adolf Hitler for my liking.

Will says that in political terms *conservative* means conserving our American Founding. Since that includes following our Declaration and Constitution, I lean toward the *conservative liberal* camp, as I mentioned previously. However, I prefer to be called a Centrist. In my last book, I defined a Centrist as someone who likes some of the ideas from the Democratic side of the aisle and some from the Republican side. Centrists do not believe either party has a lock on all the good ideas to lead our country forward. Centrists are not wishy-washy in their beliefs – we are looking for a more fiscally responsible and more socially accepting federal government. To me, it centers around civility, compassion, compromise, and common sense. I encourage you to share with your friends this definition of a

Centrist, and ask them if it is the type of leadership they would like to see from our elected officials. I predict that 60% to 80% will say "Yes."

CHAPTER 7

*Getting the Right People
in Washington*

In order to get high-quality people representing us in Washington, we first need to convince them to run for office. And for a variety of reasons that is not easy to do today:

1. To get elected, a candidate needs to obtain the financial and personnel support of either the Democratic or Republican Party. Those parties are normally led by an old guard that is very much set in its ways, so it is not easy for a newcomer to get a party endorsement. If a candidate's views are more centrist in nature – such as one looking to promote a combination of fiscal responsibility and social acceptance that the majority of people are looking for – that person would have a hard time finding a home in either party because those on the Far Left and

Far Right seem to have the most power within the parties. Unfortunately, a Centrist is not likely to change the old guard's views or get them to compromise.

2. Parties can help with some financial support, but a lot more money than that is needed to win. Therefore, a candidate needs to be a great fundraiser or personally wealthy. Few have the fundraising capabilities, and fewer have the wealth. Interestingly, the *New York Times* reported that Linda McMahon spent close to a combined $100 million of her own money in her two failed attempts to represent Connecticut, my home state, in the U.S. Senate. That is a lot of money for a $174,000 job.

3. The scrutiny that a candidate and his or her family have to go through is intense. They have to disclose to the public all their personal finances; their past is opened for the world to see; and their personal life is no longer their own. I am sure many people who would have been great representatives in Washington just did not want to put themselves and their family through such an ordeal.

Next, we need to make sure every U.S. citizen who is at least eighteen years of age can vote in free and fair elections. To do that, we must make sure it is easy for citizens to obtain the proper identification that proves their citizenship and that they live within their voting district; that there are convenient places to vote within all cities and towns; that laws against voter intimidation and discriminatory practices are enforced so they are eliminated as an obstacle to voting; and that we develop a foolproof voting system, so all Americans are confident that our election results are an accurate representation of the voters' wishes.

Then, we need to get more people to exercise their right and privilege to vote. As mentioned, I think it would make sense to combine Election Day with Veterans Day and make it one big national holiday with all businesses closed for the day. It would be the perfect way to honor our veterans who fought so hard for the freedom of all Americans, and nothing represents freedom more than voting.

What else can our country do to help get the right people in Washington? Instituting *Campaign Finance Reform*, outlawing *Gerrymandering*, replacing *Political Party Primaries* with *Top-Five Primaries*, nationalizing *Ranked Choice Voting*, and establishing *Term Limits* would be a good start.

CAMPAIGN FINANCE REFORM

If we continue on the path we are on, only the well-connected and the ultra-wealthy will be sent to Washington to represent us. That is not what our Founders had in mind, and that does not help create a more perfect Union.

Currently, individuals are allowed to donate up to $2,900 to a candidate's political campaign per election. Political Action Committees (PACs), which have been around since 1943 and raise money from donors to either support or oppose political candidates, are allowed to contribute up to $5,000 to a candidate's political campaign per election. Individuals are allowed to donate a maximum of $5,000 per year to PACs.

In the 2010 landmark case *Citizens United v. Federal Election Commission*, the Supreme Court ruled in a 5-4 decision that limiting independent spending for political communications (promotional materials, advertisements, films for or against a political candidate, etc.) by corporations, unions, and other groups violates the First Amendment right to free speech, provided they do not coordinate with, or contribute money directly to, a candidate or a political party. Unfortunately, the result has been an increase in the amount of money being spent on elections, an increase in the influence wealthy donors and organizations have on the outcome of political races, and the creation of what are called Super PACs.

Super PACs are the vehicle to take advantage of *Citizens United* as they can accept unlimited contributions from donors and have no spending restrictions. Super PACs are required to disclose the names of their donors; however, this requirement has been watered down by the fact that much of their donations comes from nonprofit organizations that do not have to disclose the names of their donors. This is referred to as *dark money* because voters do not know who is actually behind the political communications, as it is not easily traceable.

In a Brennan Center for Justice report, Daniel I. Weiner stated: "Perhaps the most troubling result of *Citizens United* [is that] in a time of historic wealth inequality, the decision has helped reinforce the growing sense that our democracy primarily serves the interests of the wealthy few, and that democratic participation for the vast majority of citizens is of relatively little value."[1] Since the Supreme Court does not have the power to create new law, even if many of its members feel a current law is not just or moral, it is up to Congress to do something about campaign finance reform and overturn *Citizens United*. Only they can create new laws and, if necessary, adopt a constitutional amendment.

In 2019, the U.S. House of Representatives passed H.R. 1, known as the *For the People Act*. One section of the Bill proposed *voluntary public financing* of federal campaigns, with a goal of making the donations from small donors more valuable than the donations from large donors by having the government match donations up to $200 at a rate of six to one. For any candidate voluntarily agreeing to participate in this program, the candidate would have to agree to not accept contributions from any one donor in excess of $1,000. This would make a six to one match added to a $200 donation the equivalent of a $1,400 donation and would make it less important for candidates to find wealthy donors. H.R. 1 did not pass in the Senate.

Strengthening the voice of small donors is critical in a representative democracy because since *Citizens United*, the wealthy have gained a disproportionate amount of power. Super PACs have now raised more than $5 billion to spend influencing elections, and of that approximately 20 percent has come from just eleven people. In addition, during the 2018 midterm elections, approximately 3,500 donors who contributed over $100,000 outspent all individual small donors – defined as donors contributing no more than $200 – who numbered at least seven million.[2] This means that large donors had 2,000 times more fundraising power than small donors.

The Brennan Center for Justice reports that one of H.R. 1's goals is to have the small donor matching program funded by a small surcharge on any criminal and civil penalties assessed to corporations that were found guilty in a court of law, with no cost to individual taxpayers. It also reports that "even if this were not the case, the price tag is exceedingly modest – roughly .01 percent of the overall federal budget over ten years."[3]

In addition to overturning *Citizens United* and creating a *voluntary public financing plan*, other ideas being discussed include banning political contributions from companies with significant foreign investments, reducing the amount a donor can contribute to a campaign, and eliminating voters from being able to contribute to races outside their own state.

In his book *A Declaration of Independents*, Greg Orman, a successful businessperson and former Independent candidate for U.S. senator in Kansas, stated the following about campaign financing: "Our system of self-government is being compromised by a campaign finance system that allows special interests to buy politicians and elections. The parties have become a duopoly and are behaving like one – dramatically limiting competition and, by extension, limiting accountability.... We are sending the worst of both parties to Washington – bitter partisans who care more about pleasing the extremists and special interests in their own party than they do moving the country forward."[4]

GERRYMANDERING

United States representatives and state legislators are elected by political districts within a state. Districts are calculated every ten years following completion of the United States census, and each district must have nearly equal populations and must not discriminate on the basis of race or ethnicity. This process is named redistricting. Gerrymandering occurs when there is manipulation of the boundaries of a voting district to favor a political party.

As David Walker states: "The purpose of redistricting should be to maximize the number of competitive districts in a manner consistent with the Voting Rights Act of 1965 rather than to minimize the number of competitive districts, as it is today. Competition is one of the key principles that made

America exceptional, and it needs to be more fully realized in our political system."[5]

According to Ballotpedia, state legislatures are responsible for redistricting the U.S. congressional districts in thirty-three states. Independent commissions determine the districts in eight states. In two states, hybrid systems are used, in which the legislatures share redistricting authority with commissions. In the remaining seven states, redistricting is not needed because they have only one district. State legislatures are responsible for redistricting state legislative districts in thirty-three states. In fourteen states, independent commissions are in charge of determining the districts. Three states use hybrid systems to establish districts.[6]

As you see, in most states the dominant political party at the time of redistricting has a great chance of picking their own voters. And it is one of the reasons over 90 percent of members of the U.S. House of Representatives and over 80 percent of U.S. senators get reelected. Because of this, I believe that all states should be required to have independent, nonpartisan commissions in charge of redistricting.

REPLACE POLITICAL PARTY PRIMARIES WITH TOP-FIVE PRIMARIES

Political party primaries are archaic and a means to take power and choice away from *We the People.* The two main parties are each controlled by a few leaders who have strong ideological views, so to win a primary a candidate must normally have to appease either the far left of the Democratic Party or the far right of the Republican Party in order to get the needed funding and support. This ensures that Centrists, like me and most

Americans, have little, if any, chance of winning a primary. This is not right and not in the best interest of the United States, because under the current rules, a lot of potentially great candidates who put "country over party" choose not to run for office.

Our country would be better served by replacing Democratic and Republican primaries in Congressional elections in each state with a single, nonpartisan primary where all candidates, whether affiliated with a party or independent, are listed on the ballot. Candidates can list their party affiliation next to their name if they choose, and all registered voters are eligible to vote in their state's primary. In their book *The Politics Industry: How Political Innovation Can Break Partisan Gridlock and Save Our Democracy*, Katherine Gehl, the former CEO of a $250 million high-tech food manufacturer and the founder of the Institute for Political Innovation, and Harvard professor Michael Porter refer to this type of primary as a Top-Five Primary because the top five finishers, regardless of party affiliation, advance to the general election. It is the first part of a two-part system named Final-Five Voting, and it would make candidates less beholden to political parties and widen the pool of good candidates interested in running for office to serve their country. In addition, it would reduce the chance of a good congressperson or senator – one who works across the political aisle and occasionally votes with the other party on a piece of legislation – from being *primaried* (the process of mounting a primary campaign against an incumbent member of Congress who has not been sufficiently partisan or did not follow the direction of his or her party's leaders).[7] Heaven forbid that our elected officials be allowed to have a mind of their own.

The second part of Final-Five Voting is replacing the type

of voting we now have in general elections – Plurality Voting, where the candidate with the most votes wins even if he or she does not have more than 50 percent of the vote – with Ranked Choice Voting (RCV).

RANKED CHOICE VOTING

Voting in our country is controlled by a duopoly – the Democratic Party and the Republican Party. They control the personnel and money normally needed to win an election. Because of that, a third-party or a fourth-party candidate has little chance of winning, so voting for one is typically a *wasted* vote. However, there is a voting system – currently being used in Maine – that eliminates any vote from being wasted. It is called Ranked Choice Voting (RCV), which is a system where voters have a ballot that allows them to rank the candidates running for office in order of their personal preference, rather than voting for only one candidate, and it could lead to better candidates choosing to run for political office.

As I mentioned earlier, I believe that 60% to 80% of people are looking for a more fiscally responsible and a more socially accepting federal government, and that combination does not fit the narrative of either of our two major political parties today. However, without RCV, it normally does not make sense to vote for candidates outside the two main parties. For example, if an environment-conscious voter votes for a Green Party candidate, who has no chance of winning, that is one less vote for the climate-conscious Democratic candidate, increasing the Republican's chance of winning. Another example would be if someone voted for a Libertarian candidate; that would likely be one less vote for the Republican candidate and increase the Democrat's chance of winning.

This is how Ranked Choice Voting works:

1. Voters go to the polls as they normally do, but instead of choosing only one candidate for an office, they rank **all** the candidates on their ballots in order of their preference.
2. If one of the candidates wins a majority of first-preference votes (over 50%), that candidate is declared the winner.
3. If no candidate wins a majority, the candidate with the fewest first-preference votes is eliminated, and the results are recalculated using the second choice of those voters whose candidate was eliminated as their *new* first-preference candidate.
4. If one of the candidates wins a majority of the retabulated first-preference votes, that candidate is declared the winner. If not, the process is repeated until one candidate wins a majority of first-preference votes.

Below is an example of the first round of balloting in an election with four candidates, 2,100 voters, and Ranked Choice Voting:

Candidate First-Preference Votes Percentage

A	675	32%
B	640	30%
C	500	24%
D	285	14%

Second Round of balloting is needed because no candidate has over 50% of the votes; D is eliminated:

Candidate First-Preference Votes Percentage

A	730	35%
B	680	32%
C	690	33%

Third Round of balloting is needed because no candidate has over 50% of the votes; B is eliminated:

Candidate First-Preference Votes Percentage

| A | 1,008 | 48% |
| C | 1,092 | 52% |

Candidate C is the declared the winner for receiving over 50% of the votes.

According to the Committee for Ranked Choice Voting, "[RCV] ensures that candidates with the most votes and broadest support win, so voters get what they want. Candidates who are opposed by a majority of voters can never win ranked choice voting elections.... Ranked choice voting levels the playing field for all candidates and encourages candidates to take their case directly to you with a focus on the issues. Candidates are encouraged to seek second choice rankings from voters whose favorite candidate is somebody else. You are less likely to rank as your second choice a candidate who has issued personal attacks against your favorite candidate."[8] Gehl and Porter state the following about RCV: "It's not just first-place votes from partisans that count. Depending on the election, candidates will have to compete to be the second or even the third choice of a much broader set of voters. Gratuitous and false negative attack ads that alienate citizens become liabilities, not roads to victory. A candidate can less easily afford to ignore swaths of the electorate when he or she needs to gain support from more than 50 percent of voters."[9]

RCV makes all the sense in the world to me, and it perfectly complements Top-Five Primaries to complete the Final-Five Voting system, a system that will help get the right people in Washington.

Term Limits

The president of the United States can serve a maximum of two four-year terms. Senators serve a six-year term with no restrictions on the number of terms. Representatives serve a two-year term with no restrictions on the number of terms. Do you think it is possible that, at times, our elected officials will make promises they know they cannot keep, or that they might vote for a piece of legislation that, though they know is not in our country's best interest, will make them look good "back home" and help their chances of getting re-elected? Do you think it is possible that someone running for office for the first time will also make promises they know they cannot keep if elected? It is not only possible; it happens all the time.

Many of our elected officials, both Democrats and Republicans, also manipulate the truth in order to make it seem that they are the only ones who can protect their constituents. A good example of this was many years ago, when I read in the newspaper that an elected official in Connecticut spoke to a group of seniors and led them to believe that they were in danger of losing Medicare benefits. They were told that the plans on the table "ask the deepest sacrifice of our seniors" and "the proposed

Medicare changes would drastically affect seniors' quality of life as payment provided by the government through the plan likely would not be enough to cover their health care costs."

This was not true because no healthcare proposal on the table at that time was to affect anyone over the age of fifty-five. My grandmother, who was 104 years old at the time, and I were not concerned that she was going to lose any of her benefits. She did not and lived to 108. This is just one example of politicians playing into the public's fears.

A few years later, this same elected official refused to review a tax article that I wrote, even though it was given to her by one of her friends and close political allies, who had read it and thought highly of it. I was told by our mutual friend that, although I was a constituent, the elected official refused to look at it because I was not affiliated with her party. Who cares what side of the aisle a good idea comes from? Apparently, many of our elected officials do, and that is sad. I guess I am not the only one to have had this problem when their elected official is from a different party. Greg Orman stated: "Many voters would find it difficult to engage in a constructive problem-solving dialogue with a candidate or officeholder of a party different from theirs. Their filters and conditioning would make it difficult for them to actively listen and seek out common ground."[10] For our nation to become all that it can be, these narrow-minded people must no longer be elected into office.

It is time for fiscal responsibility, not plans that just sound good so one can get elected or re-elected. Term limits would make telling the truth a lot easier for politicians, as no one would be worried about maintaining a lifetime job. And it would help make lobbyists much less powerful.

Because there are no term limits for elected officials other than the president, we as a nation have made it too easy to make politics a career. We need ethical, pragmatic people in office who are willing to serve our country's interests, not their own. I think we should consider having twelve years as the maximum time members of the House of Representatives and Senate can serve. Some people have suggested the idea of a one-term presidency of six years. That may not be a bad idea given how campaigns can get messy and time-consuming.

When the Constitution was written, the only federal election *We the People* were allowed to directly vote in was for our district's member in the U.S. House of Representatives. Citizens did not get to vote directly for U.S. senators or the president. Senators were chosen by state legislatures that were elected by *We the People*, and presidents were elected by electors appointed by state legislatures. Wondering why our Founders designed only a two-year term for members of the U.S. House of Representatives? Because it gave *We the People* a way to vote bad representatives out of office after only a short period of time.

As for term limits, some argue that elections are term limits because candidates can be voted in and out of office. I disagree that elections are the same as term limits. Incumbents have big advantages over a new candidate, such as having better visibility and name recognition because they can get media coverage whenever they want; they have access to government resources, such as mailings to constituents; and they can access money from their political party much more easily than a new candidate. Since incumbents in the House of Representatives win their races over 90 percent of the time, and senators win their races over 80 percent of the time, I think it is obvious that an incumbent has a much better chance of winning an election, and elections are not the equivalent of term limits.

Others argue that we need people with long-term experience down in Washington. With the gridlock and no side willing to compromise, that has not worked out too well for us in quite a while. Plus, if we get back to the limited form of government that our country was founded upon, we should not need any career politicians. We need good thinkers and good stewards rotating in and out. And this will eliminate the need for *We the People* to pay for elaborate healthcare and retirement programs for those who serve.

Once we get the right people in Washington, their task should be to not only stop Congress from shirking its responsibilities, but also to create a new set of rules for our legislative process so more gets accomplished for the benefit of *We the People*. For a long time now, I have wondered why so little gets accomplished in Washington and have asked myself a number of questions, including the following: Why do we not have a humane immigration policy that will not put a financial burden on current citizens? Since both sides of the political aisle agree that the Affordable Care Act needs to be modified and improved, why do we not yet have an improved healthcare plan? Why do we not have equality in education? Why are our children not taught about racism in U.S. history as I proposed in an earlier chapter? Why do we not have a commonsense plan to keep our environment safe, while not overloading us with costly regulations that are not proven to have positive impact?

What I have learned is that so little gets accomplished because Congress became more partisan in the early 1970s, and it has escalated to the point where today the leaders of the Democratic and Republican parties have almost all the say on what does and does not get accomplished – not Congress as a whole. Much of the problem today centers around a made-up, unwritten (not in the Constitution or the House of Representative rules book) rule that hardly anyone is aware of: *The Hastert Rule*. Gehl and Porter state the rule "dictates that the Speaker [of the House] will not allow a floor vote on a bill unless a majority of the majority party – the Speaker's party – supports the bill, *even if a majority of the full House would vote to pass it.*"[11] Consider this, even if the majority of Americans and the majority of the House of Representatives are in favor of a certain piece of legislation, but the majority of the Speaker's party is not, there is no chance of it getting passed, or even debated, because the Speaker will not allow the bill to be presented on the floor. Sadly, the Senate is managed similarly. The Hastert Rule is named after a former Speaker, and it is an abuse of power and an abomination that must be eliminated.

It would be nice to go back to the time when Congress had strong committees with influence. Committees consisted of a chairperson and members from each party. When bills were introduced to Congress, they were assigned to the appropriate committee where the members could debate the issues, offer amendments, and then decide whether to bring a bill to the floor for a vote. According to Gehl and Porter, "The committees were insulated from the parties by a set of norms, such as the seniority system, in which committee chairs were selected according to length of service, not selected with discretion by party leadership. Lacking control of personnel, party leaders had much less control over the governing process. Committees were intended to be where dialogue, deliberation, and negotiation took place and where members came together to identify problems and draft solutions."[12] What a far cry from where we are today.

CHAPTER 8

A Deeper Look into Discrimination

Racism is a form of discrimination, so it is important that we get a better understanding of the definition of discrimination and the different types of discrimination people face. When people discriminate, they are making distinctions and judgments regarding not only other people, but also things such as food, wines, and books. People with discriminating tastes are considered to be excellent judges of quality. We, of course, will focus this discussion of discrimination on the judging of people, and the impact it has on the world in which we live.

Dr. Thomas Sowell's research shows that there are three types of discrimination:[1]

1. **Discrimination IA**. This is an ability to discern differences in the qualities of people and things and choose accordingly. Decisions are based on *empirical evidence*

that, at times, can be costly to obtain. In this category of discrimination, one would *judge others individually*, regardless of what group (race, religion, gender, sexual orientation, etc.) that person belongs. This is the ideal form of discrimination, and one that you hope prospective colleges and employers use when making acceptance and hiring decisions.

2. **Discrimination IB**. This category of discrimination is used to make judgments about individuals on *empirical-based generalizations* of the specific group of people to which an individual belongs. It is used when it is deemed too costly, monetarily or otherwise, to be worth individual assessments. An example of this type of discrimination could be an employer of a company that operates dangerous machinery who is looking to hire a few employees from one of two groups. One group's membership includes 30 percent who are likely to be alcoholics, and the other group's membership includes 2 percent who are likely to be alcoholics. Evidence has shown that alcoholics are apt to produce inferior products and be a danger to themselves, fellow employees, and customers when working with dangerous machinery, so this employer does not want to hire an alcoholic. Trying to determine which of the candidates are or are not alcoholics is extremely difficult because all candidates show up sober for interviews. Given this scenario, the employer will probably use Discrimination IB and only interview people from the group with only 2 percent who are likely to be alcoholics.

3. **Discrimination II**. This category of discrimination is arbitrary or has a deep-seated bias against a group. It is

not a form of discrimination that is based on any empirical evidence. Examples include a bigoted white person thinking that he or she is superior to black people, or a male thinking that he is superior to a female. This kind of discrimination is the one we most hear about, and the use of it has led to *anti-discrimination laws and policies.*

Unfortunately, it is not practical for people to use Discrimination 1A 100 percent of the time, because although on the surface Discrimination IB makes a lot of sense, as it is less costly in time and money, the use of it has nonetheless negatively impacted young black males looking for a job. Dr. Sowell states: "A study which showed that, despite the reluctance of many employers to hire young black males, because a significant proportion of them have had criminal records, those particular employers who automatically did criminal background checks on **all** their employees tended to hire more black males than did other employers."[2] If all employers subjected applicants to a criminal background check, there would likely be more opportunities for young black males, because the vast majority of them do not have a criminal record.

Let's look at an example where Discrimination IB can impact decisions in situations other than employment concerns. Although it is a fact that most people who live in areas with a high crime rate are law-abiding, they pay a high price for the criminal minority in their neighborhood. Some businesses will not make deliveries to certain neighborhoods because they fear for their drivers' lives. Taxi drivers as well as Uber and Lyft drivers, including some black drivers, avoid driving to dangerous black neighborhoods, especially at night. Supermarkets and other businesses often have the same fears and choose not to locate stores in these known to be dangerous areas; and those willing to take the risk need to charge more for their goods and services due to higher levels of shoplifting, vandalism, burglary, and higher insurance premiums compared to similar businesses in safe neighborhoods.[3]

These examples demonstrate how a small group of unlawful citizens can have such a huge impact on the lives of a much larger group: law-abiding citizens. This needs to stop. As I stated earlier, job training for adults in poor neighborhoods so that they can develop the marketable skills necessary to become a productive member of society, and improving the education our youth receive, both in and out of the home, are needed to put our country on the path toward more peace and prosperity for all.

There is another type of discrimination that is also going on in society today. It is not as significant as what has been discussed so far in this book, but it is nonetheless important. Some call it *reverse discrimination.*

In the 1800s, Elizabeth Cady Stanton spoke of how much better life was for white men than it was for women and blacks. There are times when this continues to be true, but certainly not all. Sadly, if you are arrested, you would rather be a white male or female. Some police officers have used Discrimination IB to an extreme, and some have used Discrimination II out of sheer ignorance. We need police officers who are well-trained and treat everyone equally and with respect, particularly on traffic and other nonviolent stops. Conversely, when a police officer gives us a directive, we must follow his or her instructions. To stay safe, we must save our argument until the appropriate time – which is normally away from the incident.

However, if you are seeking acceptance into college, looking to get hired, or looking for a promotion in corporate America today, being a white man can be a disadvantage. Colleges and corporations are promoting *diversity*, which I am in favor of – when it is done properly and for the right reasons. Diversity in regard to race, religion, ethnicity, gender, and sexual orientation has many benefits in colleges and businesses, including bringing new perspectives and problem-solving techniques to the table, and having a wider pool of talent from which to select the best candidates. If students are admitted and job applicants are hired for these reasons, this is worthwhile, appropriate, and will help make not only a more perfect Union, but also a more perfect world. However, if diversity is made a priority only to meet quotas, this is discriminatory and not beneficial to society.

There have been studies showing that of the students who did not meet the normal admissions criteria at some prestigious colleges, but were admitted anyway in the name of diversity, many have not been able to handle the workload and either withdrew or flunked out. Of these students, many never again attended another college. Had these students from the start gone to a college that was a better academic fit, they would have likely graduated and had successful careers. It was not fair to put these students into a situation where they had a high probability of failure. It was not fair to the person who would have been the next person in line to be accepted. It was not fair to the other students at the college. And it was not fair to society because this person would have had a better chance of becoming a more productive member of society had he or she gone to the right college.

In the workforce today, some companies are pushing so hard to become more diversified, that gender and color are often more important than one's qualifications for the job. I know people who have been asked by their employer to hire a "type of person" rather than the best person for the job. When all things are equal or close to equal, I believe selecting someone other than a white man is appropriate when the mix of people could use a tweak. Other than that, I believe the most qualified person for the job should get the job. To do otherwise is discriminatory.

Diversity is important and beneficial to society; quotas are not. Quotas can hurt a number of people, including some of the people they are supposed to benefit. Plus, it causes a lot of resentment, which amplifies racism and does not help to repair our divided nation.

CHAPTER 9

Improving Schools

Thomas Jefferson said, "An educated citizenry is a vital requisite for our survival as a free people." We need to adhere to his advice and give all our youth a high-quality education. Earlier, I expressed what I believe needs to be taught in schools. So, how do we bring it all together to give our youth, particularly those in the inner cities, the best school experience possible?

In his quest to close "America's Education Gap," defined as the difference in the quality of education the students in the top quartile schools receive in relation to those in the bottom quartile schools, M. Night Shyamalan (writer, film director, and advocate for educational reform in the United States) researched what the best schools across the country are doing. He came up with his Five Keys needed to provide

students with the best educational experience and to eliminate the education gap. Interestingly, Shyamalan found that
there is a significant drop-off in academic performance if
not *all* Five Keys are present in the school. The Five Keys are
detailed in his book *I Got Schooled*, and below is a summary
of them:

FIRST KEY: NO ROADBLOCK TEACHERS[1]

Shyamalan's research shows that the most important key to
closing the achievement gap is increasing the odds that kids
receive great – or, at least, good – instruction for four years in
a row by making sure they do not hit a roadblock (inferior)
teacher along the way. Every school he visited that is closing
the achievement gap regularly lets go of their lowest-perform-
ing teachers.

He believes inferior teachers are costing those subjected
to inferior teachers and our country a fortune. Because of
this, schools need an accurate method of evaluating teacher
performance and value. The method found to be the best is
a combination of the review of data collected from teacher
observations and videotape, student learning growth as mea-
sured by a student's actual progress in comparison to expected
progress, and student surveys that ask the right questions, the
ones that really get at what matters inside the classroom, not
whether they like a teacher. With the elimination of tenure
and the ability of a school to be able to decide who should
no longer be teaching our children, we would be on the right
path to a more consistent, better quality educational system
in this country.

Second Key: The Right Balance of Leadership[2]

School leadership is second only to classroom teaching as an influence on learning, according to Shyamalan, and his research showed the following:

1. The most successful teams work under the most successful bosses.
2. The boss's most important job isn't communicating strategy or even hiring and firing. It is teaching skills that persist. Motivating a team of subordinates is not nearly as important as improving their skills that lead to increased productivity. Therefore, the most effective school principals are the ones who spend most of their time in the classroom observing and instructing teachers and have an operations manager to handle everything other than instruction.
3. The most effective school principals have, in closing the education gap, created a culture of high expectations in teachers and students, and provided students with a more consistent experience from year to year.

Third Key: Feedback[3]

In order to provide all children with a high-quality educational experience, Shyamalan learned that it was important to find out what was working and what was not working in one classroom, and then make sure that every classroom implemented what worked well and discarded what did not. It became evident to him that to give meaningful feedback to teachers, it was necessary to collect data regarding the curriculum, teacher technique, and student progress. He found that the feedback had to be meticulous, frequent, and mandatory, and that it had to be produced in a form that was usable because there was absolutely no evidence that collecting data had any effect until it was understandable to every teacher in a school.

Fourth Key: Smaller Schools[4]

With the principal having more of an instructional role than an administrative role, Shyamalan's research concluded that the principal would be more effective with a smaller school to oversee so he or she could spend an appropriate amount of time in each class. It also concluded that the effectiveness level of the principal drops off when the number of students in a school exceeds six hundred.

He points out that despite a common belief that there are economies-of-scale in building larger schools, his research found that it is less expensive on a per-student basis and a square-foot basis to build a school that can accommodate fewer than 725 students than it is to build one for 1,600 to 2,500 students.

Fifth Key: More Time in School[5]

Shyamalan and many others believe that American schools are not as good as they could be because they still run on a nine-teenth-century, "let's get the kids out of school so they can help with the harvest" schedule. Prior to the Civil War, Philadelphia's schools were open 250 days per year and New York's were open all year, other than a two-week break in August. That is a far cry from the 180 days we have today.

His research found that studies have been done showing children from lower-income families stayed *relatively even* with their upper-income classmates while school was in session, but fell behind dramatically every summer, with a widening gap every year thereafter. *Relatively even* in this context means that if there was a difference in aptitude, it didn't widen during the school year. One study showed it even shrunk during the school year, but the cumulative effect of summer vacations was just as damaging over the long term. This proves that children have a much better chance of academic success if they have parents who understand and teach the value of a good education and make sure their children continually improve their reading and math skills while not in school.

Fortunately, Shyamalan found that more time in school can counteract the effects of growing up in a family where education is not a priority. He feels that adding the additional hours can be accomplished in a variety of ways, such as extending the school day to 4:30, occasionally adding Saturday classes, having a shorter summer break, or instituting a mandatory three to four weeks of summer school.

In addition to the Five Keys, I believe for a couple reasons that more funds need to be earmarked for schools in poor neighborhoods. One reason is so these schools can have the ability to attract the best teachers and keep them safe. This requires giving these teachers higher salaries than their peers, and a merit system that offers even more financial rewards for outstanding performance. According to *The Economist*: "The schools that require the greatest talent often receive the most inexperienced instructors, in part because there is little financial encouragement for the best to work in them. Care in recruitment and the pairing of new instructors with experienced ones goes some way to explaining why charter schools often deliver enormous educational returns for poor black and brown children stuck in otherwise-failing urban schools. For all that teachers' unions and many on the left dislike them, charter schools that prove to be engines of opportunity should be expanded. Those that do not should have their charters revoked."[6]

The other reason for more funding is so that children living in high-poverty neighborhoods can be served a free breakfast and lunch. These children often come to school hungry, and it is difficult for a hungry child to learn. It is also difficult to teach a hungry child. This is something children and teachers in more affluent school districts normally do not have to deal with, but this nutritional problem is weighing down a part of America that needs to be lifted up so they can become contributing members of society. If providing funds only to schools located in high-poverty neighborhoods so they can offer free breakfast and lunch and attract high-quality teachers does not seem fair, remember that *equal is not always equitable*.

I also believe schools need to demand discipline from their students. Just as you can only make a first impression once, you can only get a traditional K-12 education once. By traditional, I am referring to starting at approximately five years old and ending at approximately eighteen years old. To become economically self-reliant, children need to get all they can out of their educational experience, and classmates who are disruptive limit the amount that can be learned.

Dr. Sowell was not a fan of President George W. Bush's "no child left behind" initiative because he believes, "When a handful of disruptive or violent students can prevent a whole class from getting a decent education, such students must be separated – 'left behind' – if the others are not to be denied an education, which may be their one chance for a better life.... The need to separate disruptive or violent children from others who are trying to learn is independent of whether or not there is any 'solution' currently available, or on the horizon, for changing the behavior of disruptive and/or violent children. The alternative is to sacrifice the education of unending generations of poor and minority children until such indefinite time as a 'solution' for their misbehaving and/or violent classmates can be found, created or faked.... None of this precludes trying to improve the behavior of problem students. It simply does not postpone the education of a whole generation of other students until that project succeeds."[7] I agree with Dr. Sowell, and I believe that well-nourished students will cause fewer problems in the classroom.

CHAPTER 10

Income and Wealth Inequality

The income and wealth gap between the top and bottom tier of society is stark – some say dangerously stark. The question is, should narrowing the gap be one of our country's top priorities? Let's look into that.

To answer the question, we first need to understand why our ancestors came to America. Sadly, some of our ancestors were forced to come to America as slaves, but most chose to come to this great, but not perfect, country because they felt they had a better opportunity to create the life they wanted for themselves and their families here than in their homeland.

Many of our ancestors were trying to leave a country where they were not free to own property and profit from the land, where hard work was not rewarded, and where economic and personal success were not readily attainable. Many wanted to leave a country where they were not allowed their own freedom of expression or thought because of tyrannical governments. Many others wanted to leave a country where they were not allowed to worship as they saw fit.

The countries many of our ancestors left had governments that were run only by a select few with no power held by *We the People*. They did not have a representative form of government with limited powers. Some of the governments owned the land and businesses, so all but a relatively few people were dependent on the government for food, income, healthcare, and shelter.

Our ancestors came to America seeking freedom. They wanted to live, work, and worship the way they chose, and to escape controlling bureaucratic governments. They wanted the opportunity to create the life of their dreams, although there were no guarantees, as well as the opportunity for self-actualization through hard work. They wanted to have the opportunity for earned success that brings the dignity Nitin Nohria speaks of – becoming economically self-reliant. This is **the pursuit of Happiness** that is stated in our Declaration of Independence.

Harvard professor Arthur Brooks feels similarly to Dr. Nohria. Brooks says in his book *The Road to Freedom,* that the path our ancestors were on was the Free Enterprise System, which he describes as a "system of values and laws that respects private property and limits government, encourages competition and industry, celebrates achievement based on merit, and creates individual opportunity."[1] He also states that "succeeding on merit, doing something meaningful, seeing the poor rise by their hard work and virtue, and having control over life are essential to happiness and fulfillment."[2]

Although I believe that the free enterprise system is by far the best economic system known to man and has lifted up more people from poverty than any other economic system, it must always be coupled with a *safety net* for our least fortunate members of society. This safety net must provide for the well-being of those who are not physically or mentally capable of providing for themselves. This combination of free enterprise and a safety net is both fair and moral.

Once we understand that we Americans are happiest when we are striving for economic self-reliance, we then need to ask ourselves if our society gives all citizens an equal opportunity, and more importantly an equal chance, of becoming economically self-reliant. I hope I have proven to you that because not all students in our nation are receiving a high-quality education in our public school systems, not all citizens have an equal chance of success, and I hope you agree with me that this failure in our country needs to be addressed.

Dr. Thomas Sowell has traveled the world studying the subject of success and has determined the following:[3]

1. Family background matters. Children of parents who went to college and stress the ***importance of education*** have an advantage. Children growing up with both parents living under one roof have an advantage. Children exposed to over 2,000 words per day have an advantage over those who are exposed to 1,000 or fewer words per day.

2. Social background matters. People from different social backgrounds may have different goals and priorities. For example, not everyone has the same desire to *move up* in society, and some cultures have had more of a desire than others. According to Sowell, those with a ***desire to succeed*** at something specific, a willingness to ***do what it takes***, and ***some natural ability*** have the best chance of success.

3. Prerequisites matter. For whatever endeavor you want to succeed in, you must figure out what the prerequisites are to succeed in that particular endeavor, and you must learn or satisfy *all* of them. Whether success in your endeavor requires three, five, or ten prerequisites, all must be learned or satisfied in order to succeed.

I believe Dr. Sowell's points should be looked at in a positive light rather than a negative one, because they define the most important things needed to succeed. His message should be looked upon as a **Success Roadmap** that includes the roadblocks that will need to be avoided or overcome. Not all of our parents went to college. Mine didn't, but they worked hard and instinctively knew that a high-quality education is one of the keys to success and emphasized that to my sister and me. They emphasized it so much, that many years after my sister and I graduated from college, my mother went on earn her degree while working a full-time job. Not all of us are surrounded by good role models, but with a desire to succeed and a willingness to work hard, one can achieve personal success. This is proven by the stories of millions of people who overcame great odds to reach their goals.

Not all of us have all the prerequisites needed to succeed in our chosen endeavor. When this is the case, we need to accept the fact and choose another one. I had to. Although I wanted to play professional baseball like my grandfather, and I had a modicum of success, there were prerequisites I could not overcome, such as a lack of speed, arm strength, and power. My coaches can verify this.

Interestingly, Sowell states: "Given multiple prerequisites for many human endeavors, we should not be surprised if economic or social advances are not evenly or randomly distributed among individuals, groups, institutions or nations at any given time. Nor should we be surprised if the laggards in one century forge ahead in some later century, or if world leaders in one era become laggards in another era. When the gain or loss of just one prerequisite can turn failure into success or turn success into failure, it should not be surprising, in a changing world, if the leaders and laggards of one century or millennium exchange places in some later century or millennium."[4]

Because family is so important to one's quality of life and the success one has in life, I hope you enjoy the following story:

On the Sunday after Christmas in 2015, my wife and I were in New York City, and we decided to go to St. Patrick's Cathedral to hear Cardinal Timothy Dolan give Mass. When Cardinal Dolan entered from the rear of the church, you thought you were at a rock concert. He was high-fiving and hugging people as he walked up the aisle to the alter. It was very exciting, even for me, a non-Catholic who grew up attending a Methodist church.

The cardinal's message that day started with a question. "The two most important words in a family begin with the letter *M*—what are they?" A few people blurted out their guesses, and not surprisingly the most popular one was "mother." Finally, he announced that "mother" is indeed one of the two most important words in a family, because without a mother a family could never get started. He also announced that no one correctly guessed the second word, which he informed us is "meal." Cardinal Dolan and many others believe that families do not sit down together for enough meals. He believes that so much is learned when a family sits down together to eat because when families gather around the table, people have the opportunity to communicate. Cardinal Dolan and many others also believe that a lack of family meals – often because of today's fast-paced world – has been a major contributor to the breakdown of the family unit and has greatly damaged our society.

Cardinal Dolan's message resonated with me because breakfast and dinner were oftentimes the only part of the day that my whole family was together when I was a child. It was our time to discuss what everyone was doing, any successes one had, any problems someone in the family may be having that needed to be addressed, current events in the world, and have some laughs. For us it was a great time to bond. However, for many families it is not always possible to get together for meals, and that is okay. I think what he was really saying is that families need more "family time." That could be spending time together playing games, going out for ice cream, walking the dog, or anything else you can think of to do as a family. The important thing is spending time together.

Let's now go back to the question I posed at the beginning of this chapter: Should narrowing the income and wealth gap be one of our country's top priorities? In his book *Wealth, Poverty and Politics,* Dr. Thomas Sowell looks at the situation this way: "If the less fortunate peoples of the world are less fortunate primarily because they are victims of the more fortunate, then the goal to pursue in trying to make things right can be very different from what the goal would be if the less fortunate are seen as people lacking the geographic, cultural and other advantages enjoyed by others, largely through no fault of theirs or of others."[5] So it really comes down to which problem is more important to solve:

1. The reduction or elimination of economic gaps between people, or
2. Spreading prosperity to all people by making sure

everyone has the opportunity to learn the skills and behaviors necessary for economic success.

Many people may feel the above are complementary goals and want to accomplish both. However, consider this: If everyone's skills were improved and their income doubled – which would be a good thing if purchasing power remained the same because it would reduce the number of people living in poverty – it would increase the income and wealth gap in society. Given that scenario, I would argue that finding a way to spread prosperity is a more important goal than one that attempts to solve the income and wealth inequality issue. That said, I believe that the compensation of CEOs at the world's largest corporations is too high in relation to the value they provide their respective companies, and excessive in relation to the pay of rank-and-file employees. I also believe that some changes can be made to the U.S. Tax Code to make it more equitable, and I will address some of these in the next chapter.

A couple things you should note:

1. Income disparity is not always the best indicator of economic disparity. Standard of living is a better indicator. According to Sowell, "In the United States, most households in the lowest 20 percent of income recipients have **no one** working. Most of the economic resources transferred to them are transferred in kind – subsidized housing, medical care and other such benefits – rather than in money. Therefore, disparities expressed in money income statistics greatly exaggerate disparities in standards of living, especially for people living in what the welfare state chooses to define as poverty."[6]

2. Sowell argues that the majority of statistical studies

regarding income trends are not the most accurate. One type of study breaks down into quintiles the income levels of the population each year and then compares the data with other years. This study is straightforward and easy to calculate as there is no concern for the fact that there is an ever-changing mix of people in each quintile. Statistics from this study are what the media, politicians, and academic world most often cite. Sowell believes the other type of study, which follows the changes of the annual income of identical individuals over many years, is more costly but a more accurate measure as to what is happening with people's incomes. Why is this? Because people move from one quintile to another in the normal course of their careers, getting paid much more once they are experienced than when they started out. Logically, people in their fifties and sixties normally get paid a lot more than someone in their twenties.[7] I think it is obvious that the second type of study gives a more accurate assessment of where our population is economically.

A reduction in the income and wealth inequality we have in society would still leave many below the poverty line. Therefore, our government's efforts should be channeled toward assuring that every child has access to a great education, and that every adult has access to the retraining needed to develop the skills necessary to earn, at least, a living wage and be able to succeed in our ever-changing work environment. Since those who lack the most basic things in life would certainly benefit the most from improved skills and a rise in income, I believe our government's efforts should be channeled in this direction, and less on the income and wealth gap.

CHAPTER 11

America's Unsustainable Fiscal Path

No book regarding the creation of a more perfect Union for all citizens would be complete without a discussion about our country's finances. The following is extremely important information that all Americans need to know.

The following financially astute people and organizations have all stated that our federal government has put the United States on an unsustainable fiscal path: Federal Reserve Chairman Jerome Powell; former Federal Reserve Chairmen Ben Bernanke and Alan Greenspan; the Government Accountability Office (GAO); and the International Monetary Fund (IMF). This should cause you great concern because if our fiscal problems are not addressed, our children and all future generations may end up living in a country none of us could have ever imagined.

In the Preamble to the Constitution of the United States of America, the law of our land, it tasks *We the People* with the job of securing the Blessings of Liberty for ourselves and our Posterity. This means that we are required by law to make sure that all future generations are free from oppressive restrictions imposed by any so-called authority from within our country or from outside our borders. For this to happen, America needs to be strong economically, diplomatically, and militarily. David Walker states: "History clearly shows that the most important factor in achieving and maintaining great power or super-power status is economic power....Economic strength brings diplomatic influence and enables military power."[1] We must maintain our economic advantage over the rest of the world and make sure our dollar continues to be the ***world's reserve currency***, the most trusted and most redeemable currency for facilitating world commerce. Unfortunately, this is becoming a more and more difficult task, as our annual ***federal deficits*** are increasing, and our ***national debt*** continues to grow.

Admiral Bill Owens, United States Navy (retired) and former vice chairman of the Joint Chiefs of Staff, believes that our country's growing debt burden is the greatest national security threat because we need to be able to fund a strong military to "face a myriad of changing security threats that are arguably greater than any we have faced since World War II."[2] He also states that it is "very important for our country to maintain a strong military to ensure the preservation of our agenda of freedom, human rights, democratic principles, free and fair trade, and the protection of the other values and interests of the American people."[3] Sadly, you will not hear much about this from many of our elected officials in Washington, and that is likely for one of two reasons:

1. They would have to admit that our country's financial problems started decades ago, that they added to the problem by doing nothing to fix it, and because of that they fear their constituents would get angry and vote them out of office; or

2. They believe *We the People* are too ignorant to be able to handle the truth.

These are not good reasons for those in Washington to shirk their responsibility, and they are insulting to the American voters. It is time for Washington to educate the public, because if we are going to pass on the Blessings of Liberty to all future generations of Americans, something our Founders wanted and expected us to do, we all need to understand the impact deficits and debt have on society, and we need to demand that our elected officials in Washington address these issues as soon as possible.

Do not let your political biases fool you; both political parties are to blame for our country's financial problems. Republicans normally do not want to raise taxes, even when our country is in need of more revenue. And Democrats normally do not want to reduce spending, even though our country has been on an unsustainable fiscal path for a long period of time. It seems as though the only party to speak about our nation's financial woes is the party that is not in power. And once they get back into power, they forge ahead with their own agenda and put fiscal responsibility on the back burner.

When I want the facts about America's financial situation, I look to David Walker, and so should our elected officials. Mr. Walker is a CPA who has worked in the private, public, and nonprofit arenas; he headed the Pension Benefit Guaranty

Corporation; he was appointed by President Reagan to be Assistant Secretary of Labor for Pension and Welfare Benefit Programs; he was appointed by President George H. W. Bush to be one of two public trustees of the Social Security and Medicare trust funds; he was appointed by President Clinton in 1998 to be the Comptroller General of the United States and continued in that role under President George W. Bush until 2008; he is the author of four books, including *Comeback America* and his latest book, *America in 2040: Still a Superpower?*; and he is currently a professor at the United States Naval Academy. In his role as Comptroller General, Walker was essentially the Auditor General and Chief Accountability Officer for the federal government and the CEO of the Government Accountability Office.

According to Walker:[4]

1. As of June 30, 2020, our federal/national debt was $26.48 trillion and rising. This is made up of the total amount of U.S. Treasury issued debt that is held by individuals; private pension plans and trusts; federal government trust funds, such as Social Security and Medicare; central banks from all over the world; and other entities. Of the $26.48 trillion, $20.53 trillion was held by the public, and $5.95 trillion was held by federal government trust funds.

2. At the end of Fiscal Year 2019, our nation's unfunded liabilities for Social Security and Medicare were around $59 trillion and growing. These liabilities are calculated by taking the present value of the difference between the projected total payments and expenses of these programs over the next seventy-five years and the amount of projected revenues these programs (i.e., payroll taxes) will

generate over the next seventy-five years. Present value is defined as the amount of money needed to be invested today, so that at a given rate of return it will grow to meet future needs.

3. Our Fiscal Year 2019 federal spending consisted of approximately 70% going to Mandatory Expenditures and 30% to Discretionary Expenditures. Mandatory Expenditures are determined by statutory eligibility requirements and benefit formulas, and include Social Security, Medicare, Medicaid, income security programs, agricultural subsidies, and interest on our federal debt. These expenditures are locked in place unless there is a change in statute. Discretionary Expenditures are determined by an annual appropriations process, and in Fiscal Year 2019 approximately half went to Defense spending, and the balance went to a variety of different departments and programs. Please refer to the chart below:

Federal Spending, FY 2019

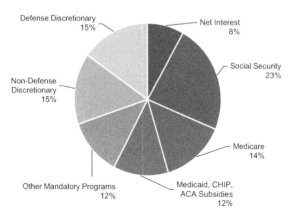

Note: Figures may not add to 100% due to rounding

Source: Office of Management and Budget

Because interest rates have been at historic lows, the annual interest payment on our debt has not yet become a big problem. However, our debt level continues to grow, and interest costs are the fastest growing recurring expense in our federal budget. When interest rates go up, and eventually they will, the interest on our federal debt will become a serious problem. Walker states: "If interest rates were to return to pre-2007 financial crisis levels, that would result in additional interest costs on federal debt of $800 billion per year."[5] I shudder to think what the total interest cost will be at higher debt levels, because the more we pay for interest costs, the less money we will have for Social Security, Medicare, and other important programs, and the more our children and all future generations will have to pay for our mistakes.

The percentage of discretionary spending within our overall budget has been coming down for many years, with most of the decline coming from spending for national defense. As stated earlier, discretionary spending is now only about 30%; however, it was 40% in Fiscal Year 2010. The decline is projected to continue because mandatory spending is projected to rise for the following reasons:[6]

1. A reduction in the worker-to-retiree ratio will adversely affect Social Security.
2. Increasing health care costs will adversely affect Medicare and other health-related programs.
3. The rise in interest costs as our debt level increases and interest rates inch higher.

It is obvious that our government has a spending problem, and that for many years now our elected officials have not been good leaders or good stewards of the money they collect from *We the People* through taxation. Unless we want to leave our future generations in such financial peril that our country would be vulnerable to attacks by another country, such as China or Russia, that does not believe in and support the values established by our Founders, our elected officials need to stop being concerned about getting re-elected and start making the difficult decisions needed to set us on a sustainable fiscal path.

These difficult decisions need to come after a thorough analysis is done by a nonpartisan audit committee that does a deep-dive into all mandatory and discretionary federal expenditures, including Social Security and Medicare since they are a large percentage of the budget. Our country is in desperate need of such a committee. I know that may sound alarming because these are two very important programs for the elderly, but analysis does not mean elimination. We just need to make sure these plans are actuarily sound, and do not bankrupt future generations.

Regarding Social Security, the Congressional Budget Office (CBO) estimates that because of COVID-19, the combined OASDI Trust Funds are expected to be exhausted in 2032, three years earlier than the 2020 Annual Social Security Trustees Report projected. Medicare has two trust funds, one for Part A and one for Parts B, C, and D, and only Part A is in danger of running out of money. The 2020 Medicare Trustees Report estimated that would happen in 2026, but because of COVID-19, the CBO now estimates that it will be in 2023.[7]

I hope these sobering statistics have concerned you enough to read more about our nation's finances and what they mean to you, your heirs, and the future of our nation. If they have, I highly recommend you read David Walker's book *America in 2040: Still a Superpower?* He not only lays out the problems we face, but he also has some possible solutions, and he should definitely be on the nonpartisan audit committee I am calling for.

As promised, I will share some ideas I have regarding our U.S. Tax Code. Given the size of our national debt, our federal government needs to not only reduce spending, but it also needs to increase revenue. With this in mind, I think we should consider the following:

1. Carried interest should not get special tax treatment. I fail to see why investment managers of *private equity funds* are allowed to have the income they earn from managing other people's money taxed at the more favorable long-term capital gains rates rather than at the ordinary income rates the rest of us pay on our earned income.

2. Stock options are a form of executive compensation that converts ordinary income into long-term capital gains and are a huge tax benefit for wealthy CEOs at major corporations. The fairness and usefulness of this form of compensation should be studied.

3. Change the taxation of dividends. Investors who receive dividends from U.S. corporations are taxed at long-term capital gains rates rather than at ordinary income rates. Part of the rationale for this is that when corporations pay a dividend, it is not a tax-deductible expense and is, therefore, paid from a pool of money that has already been taxed. However, many people believe that investment income should not be taxed at lower rates than income earned through employment. A possible solution would be to continue having corporations pay dividends from after-tax money, but only allow people with taxable income below a designated threshold to have

their dividends taxed at the favorable long-term capital gains rates. Those with taxable income above the threshold would have their dividends taxed as ordinary income.

4. Increase the number of brackets used to calculate the tax on ordinary income and raise the top rate to 50%. At what level of income would I consider taxing people at 50%? Maybe at $1,000,000, $2,500,000, $5,000,000, or some other amount. The Tax Plan I proposed in *Politics Beyond Left and Right* was based on the premise that the middle class needs to keep more of its income, and that small-business owners provide the majority of jobs in this country, so they should not be burdened with excessive taxes that make it difficult for them to expand and create more good-paying jobs. I believe that since the majority of small-business owners make less than $500,000 per year, anyone making less than that should not incur an increase in taxes.

5. Maintain the tax preference long-term capital gains receive. Capital investments include investments in businesses that provide needed products and services, and create jobs. Examples include manufacturing, construction, retail, financial services, and technology companies. Home ownership is also a capital investment. I believe that the profits people make on capital investments held for longer than one year should continue to be taxed at long-term capital gains rates, not ordinary income rates, because capital investments are good for society. People invest their own hard-earned money that has already been taxed, they risk losing it all, and they only profit if their investment is worth more at the time of sale. If you sell a capital investment this year that you have owned

for twenty years and has appreciated $200,000, it is very different than if you got paid a $200,000 salary that was earned in one year. It took you twenty years to realize a one-time profit of $200,000 on this capital investment. That is the equivalent of only $10,000 per year. Capital gains deserve tax preference status, and I believe the highest rate should be capped at 25%.

Instituting these tax initiatives would not come close to solving our country's fiscal problems, but it is a step in the right direction and the optics would be helpful in unifying our nation. The audit commission I am calling for can determine the best course of action and whether these revenue-generating ideas make sense.

In summary, we need our federal government and state governments to become fiscally responsible, so we do not leave future generations of Americans vulnerable and in financial peril. It is time to get America on a sustainable fiscal path!

Conclusion

I hope my desire for a more perfect Union resonates with you, and that you agree with the following:

- That we need to overcome America's biggest mistake – our country's leaders during and shortly after Reconstruction not adhering to our Constitution – so our nation can become the "shining city on a hill" that John F. Kennedy and Ronald Reagan sought, one that is more peaceful and prosperous for all.
- That it is time for a world that is filled with more civility, compassion, compromise, and common sense.
- That it is time to end the identification and division of people by race, religion, political beliefs, gender, or sexual orientation.
- That it is time for every American to buy into the idea that

all Americans need to be guaranteed that they have not just an opportunity, but also a real chance, at becoming economically self-reliant and living a life with dignity... and then do all they can do to help make it a reality.

- That it is time to implement the changes in our school curriculum that I proposed, so all Americans gain a deep understanding about our nation's Founding; learn how our Declaration of Independence and our Constitution are inseparable and still relevant today; discover what role each of us has in helping America become a more perfect Union; and gain exposure to not only our country's triumphs but also our failures, so the mistakes of the past are never again repeated. We must learn from our past, not run from it, because when we take the time to understand the past, we are then in a better position to improve the present and the future.

- That it is time for the American people to finally prove to Frederick Douglass that we do have loyalty enough, honor enough, and patriotism enough to live up to our Constitution.

- That it is time for Supreme Court justices not to let personal beliefs and values factor into how they rule on a case brought before them. They are there to render decisions based on law, not to create law.

- That it is time for Congress to stop abdicating its responsibilities, adhere to the separation of powers our Founders instituted, and legislate.

- That it is time to implement both parts of Final-Five Voting (Top-Five Primaries and Ranked Choice Voting) and create a new set of rules for our legislative process so more gets accomplished for the benefit of *We the People*.

- That it is time for Congress to follow James Madison's message in "Federalist 62" to write comprehensible legislation: "It will be of little avail to the people, that the laws are made by men of their own choice, if the laws be so voluminous that they cannot be read, or so incoherent that they cannot be understood."
- That it is time for more liberal thinkers in Washington – ones who are willing to work across the aisle because no one party has a lock on all the best ideas, and ones who are more concerned about doing what is best for *We the People* than they are in getting reelected. For this to happen, something needs to be done to prevent leaders of political parties from pressuring their colleagues in Congress to vote along party lines.
- That our federal government needs to be fiscally responsible so future generations are not put in financial peril.

I hope I have proven to you that when our country's leaders during a critical period in U.S. history did not adhere to the Constitution, it set a bad precedent that gave the false impression to future leaders that it is permissible not to adhere to the Constitution when it does not meet their personal beliefs and agenda. This precedent has had grave consequences, particularly for people of color. Since our Constitution is the supreme Law of the Land, it is illegal not to adhere to it. This nonadherence set our nation on a destructive path that has often steered our leaders away from our Founders' vision.

I believe Professor Carol Anderson summarizes Reconstruction best: "Imagine if Reconstruction had actually honored the citizenship of four million freed people – provided the education, political autonomy, and economic wherewithal warranted by their and their ancestors' hundreds of years of free labor. If, instead of continually fighting the Civil War, we had actually moved on to rebuilding a strong, viable South, a South where poor whites, too – for they had been left out as well – could gain access to proper education....We shouldn't have to imagine."[1]

I believe in Dr. Martin Luther King, Jr.'s dream to live in a nation where people are not judged by the color of their skin – and I'll add religion, gender, sexual orientation, or political beliefs – but by the content of their character. I have never given any of those a thought when determining whether I liked someone, and I wish the world felt the same.

What follows are four of the most important documents in America's history: Dr. Martin Luther King, Jr.'s "Letter from a Birmingham Jail," the Declaration of Independence, the Constitution of the United States of America, and the Amendments to the Constitution of the United States of America. I encourage you to read them when you have the time to do a deep dive into understanding each document's message. I think you will be impressed.

To a more perfect Union!

"Letter from a Birmingham Jail"

by Dr. Martin Luther King, Jr.

16 April 1963

My Dear Fellow Clergymen:

While confined here in the Birmingham city jail, I came across your recent statement calling my present activities "unwise and untimely." Seldom do I pause to answer criticism of my work and ideas. If I sought to answer all the criticisms that cross my desk, my secretaries would have little time for anything other than such correspondence in the course of the day, and I would have no time for constructive work. But since I feel that you are men of genuine good will and that your criticisms are sincerely set forth, I want to try to answer your statement in what I hope will be patient and reasonable terms.

I think I should indicate why I am here in Birmingham, since you have been influenced by the view which argues against "outsiders coming in." I have the honor of serving as president of the Southern Christian Leadership Conference, an organization operating in every southern state, with headquarters in Atlanta, Georgia. We have some eighty five affiliated organizations across the South, and one of them is the Alabama Christian Movement for Human Rights. Frequently we share staff, educational and financial resources with our affiliates. Several months ago the affiliate here in Birmingham asked us to be on call to engage in a nonviolent direct action program if such were deemed necessary. We readily consented, and when the hour came we lived up to our promise. So I, along with several members of my staff, am here because I was invited here. I am here because I have organizational ties here.

But more basically, I am in Birmingham because injustice is here. Just as the prophets of the eighth century B.C. left their villages and carried their "thus saith the Lord" far beyond the boundaries of their home towns, and just as the Apostle Paul left his village of Tarsus and carried the gospel of Jesus Christ to the far corners of the Greco Roman world, so am I compelled to carry the gospel of freedom beyond my own home town. Like Paul, I must constantly respond to the Macedonian call for aid.

Moreover, I am cognizant of the interrelatedness of all communities and states. I cannot sit idly by in Atlanta and not be concerned about what happens in Birmingham. Injustice anywhere is a threat to justice everywhere. We are caught in an inescapable network of mutuality, tied in a single garment of destiny. Whatever affects one directly, affects all indirectly. Never again can we afford to live with the narrow, provincial "outside agitator" idea. Anyone who lives inside the United States can never be considered an outsider anywhere within its bounds.

You deplore the demonstrations taking place in Birmingham. But your statement, I am sorry to say, fails to express a similar concern for the conditions that brought about the demonstrations. I am sure that none of you would want to rest content with the superficial kind of social analysis that deals merely with effects and does not grapple with underlying causes. It is unfortunate that demonstrations are taking place in Birming-ham, but it is even more unfortunate that the city's white power structure left the Negro community with no alternative.

In any nonviolent campaign there are four basic steps: collec-tion of the facts to determine whether injustices exist; negotia-tion; self purification; and direct action. We have gone through all these steps in Birmingham. There can be no gainsaying the fact that racial injustice engulfs this community. Birmingham is probably the most thoroughly segregated city in the United States. Its ugly record of brutality is widely known. Negroes have experienced grossly unjust treatment in the courts. There have been more unsolved bombings of Negro homes and churches in Birmingham than in any other city in the nation. These are the hard, brutal facts of the case. On the basis of these conditions, Negro leaders sought to negotiate with the city fathers. But the latter consistently refused to engage in good faith negotiation.

Then, last September, came the opportunity to talk with leaders of Birmingham's economic community. In the course of the negotiations, certain promises were made by the mer-chants—for example, to remove the stores' humiliating racial signs. On the basis of these promises, the Reverend Fred Shuttlesworth and the leaders of the Alabama Christian Move-ment for Human Rights agreed to a moratorium on all demon-strations. As the weeks and months went by, we realized that we were the victims of a broken promise. A few signs, briefly removed, returned; the others remained. As in so many past experiences, our hopes had been blasted, and the shadow of deep disappointment settled upon us. We had no alternative except to prepare for direct action, whereby we would present our very bodies as a means of laying our case before the conscience of the local and the national community. Mindful of the difficulties involved, we decided to undertake a process of self purification. We began a series of workshops on nonviolence, and we repeatedly asked ourselves: "Are you able to accept blows without retaliating?" "Are you able to endure the ordeal of jail?" We decided to schedule our direct action program for the Easter season, realizing that except for Christmas, this is the main shopping period of the year. Knowing that a strong economic-withdrawal program would be the by product of direct action, we felt that this would be the best time to bring pressure to bear on the merchants for the needed change.

Then it occurred to us that Birmingham's mayoral election was coming up in March, and we speedily decided to postpone action until after election day. When we discovered that the Commissioner of Public Safety, Eugene "Bull" Connor, had piled up enough votes to be in the run off, we decided again to postpone action until the day after the run off so that the demonstrations could not be used to cloud the issues. Like many others, we waited to see Mr. Connor defeated, and to this end we endured postponement after postponement. Having aided in this community need, we felt that our direct action program could be delayed no longer.

You may well ask: "Why direct action? Why sit ins, marches and so forth? Isn't negotiation a better path?" You are quite right in calling for negotiation. Indeed, this is the very purpose of direct action. Nonviolent direct action seeks to create such a crisis and foster such a tension that a community which has constantly refused to negotiate is forced to confront the issue. It seeks so to dramatize the issue that it can no longer be ignored. My citing the creation of tension as part of the work of the nonviolent resister may sound rather shocking. But I must confess that I am not afraid of the word "tension." I have earnestly opposed violent tension, but there is a type of constructive, nonviolent tension which is necessary for growth. Just as Socrates felt that it was necessary to create a tension in the mind so that individuals could rise from the bondage of myths and half truths to the unfettered realm of creative analysis and objective appraisal, so must we see the need for nonviolent gadflies to create the kind of tension in society that will help men rise from the dark depths of prejudice and racism to the majestic heights of understanding and brotherhood. The purpose of our direct action program is to create a situation so crisis packed that it will inevitably open the door to negotiation. I therefore concur with you in your call for negotiation. Too long has our beloved Southland been bogged down in a tragic effort to live in monologue rather than dialogue.

One of the basic points in your statement is that the action that I and my associates have taken in Birmingham is untimely. Some have asked: "Why didn't you give the new city administration time to act?" The only answer that I can give to this query is that the new Birmingham administration must be prodded about as much as the outgoing one, before it will act. We are sadly mistaken if we feel that the election of Albert Boutwell as mayor will bring the millennium to Birmingham. While Mr. Boutwell is a much more gentle person than Mr. Connor, they are both segregationists, dedicated to maintenance of the status quo. I have hope that Mr. Boutwell will be reasonable enough to see the futility of massive resistance to desegregation. But he will not see this without pressure from devotees of civil rights. My friends, I must say to you that we have not made a single gain in civil rights without determined legal and nonviolent pressure. Lamentably, it is an historical fact that privileged groups seldom give up their privileges voluntarily. Individuals may see the moral light and voluntarily give up their unjust posture; but, as Reinhold Niebuhr has reminded us, groups tend to be more immoral than individuals.

We know through painful experience that freedom is never voluntarily given by the oppressor; it must be demanded by the oppressed. Frankly, I have yet to engage in a direct action campaign that was "well timed" in the view of those who have not suffered unduly from the disease of segregation. For years now I have heard the word "Wait!" It rings in the ear of every Negro with piercing familiarity. This "Wait" has almost always meant "Never." We must come to see, with one of our distinguished jurists, that "justice too long delayed is justice denied."

We have waited for more than 340 years for our constitutional and God given rights. The nations of Asia and Africa are moving with jetlike speed toward gaining political independence, but we still creep at horse and buggy pace toward gaining a cup of coffee at a lunch counter. Perhaps it is easy for those who have never felt the stinging darts of segregation to say, "Wait." But when you have seen vicious mobs lynch your mothers and fathers at will and drown your sisters and brothers at whim; when you have seen hate filled policemen curse, kick and even kill your black brothers and sisters; when you see the vast majority of your twenty million Negro brothers smothering in an airtight cage of poverty in the midst of an affluent society; when you suddenly find your tongue twisted and your speech stammering as you seek to explain to your six year old daughter why she can't go to the public amusement park that has just been advertised on television, and see tears welling up in her eyes when she is told that Funtown is closed to colored children, and see ominous clouds of inferiority beginning to form in her little mental sky, and see her beginning to distort her personality by developing an unconscious bitterness toward white people; when you have to concoct an answer for a five year old son who is asking: "Daddy, why do white people treat colored people so mean?"; when you take a cross county drive and find it necessary to sleep night after night in the uncomfortable corners of your automobile because no motel will accept you; when you are humiliated day in and day out by nagging signs reading "white" and "colored"; when your first name becomes "nigger," your middle name becomes "boy" (however old you are) and your last name becomes "John," and your wife and mother are never given the respected title "Mrs."; when you are harried by day and haunted by night by the fact that you are a Negro, living constantly at tiptoe stance, never quite knowing what to expect next, and are plagued with inner fears and outer resentments; when you are forever fighting a degenerating sense of "nobodiness"—then you will understand why we find it difficult to wait. There comes a time when the cup of endurance runs over, and men are no longer willing to be plunged into the abyss of despair. I hope, sirs, you can understand our legitimate and unavoidable impatience. You express a great deal of anxiety over our willingness to break laws. This is certainly a legitimate concern. Since we so diligently urge people to obey the Supreme Court's decision of 1954 outlawing segregation in the public schools, at first glance it may seem rather paradoxical for us consciously to break laws. One may well ask: "How can you advocate breaking some laws and obeying others?" The answer lies in the fact that there are two types of laws: just and unjust. I would be the first to advocate obeying just laws. One has not only a legal but a moral responsibility to obey just laws. Conversely, one has a moral responsibility to disobey unjust laws. I would agree with St. Augustine that "an unjust law is no law at all."

Now, what is the difference between the two? How does one determine whether a law is just or unjust? A just law is a man made code that squares with the moral law or the law of God. An unjust law is a code that is out of harmony with the moral law. To put it in the terms of St. Thomas Aquinas: An unjust law is a human law that is not rooted in eternal law and natural law. Any law that uplifts human personality is just. Any law that degrades human personality is unjust. All segregation statutes are unjust because segregation distorts the soul and damages the personality. It gives the segregator a false sense of superiority and the segregated a false sense of inferiority. Segregation, to use the terminology of the Jewish philosopher Martin Buber, substitutes an "I it" relationship for an "I thou" relationship and ends up relegating persons to the status of things. Hence segregation is not only politically, economically and sociologically unsound, it is morally wrong and sinful. Paul Tillich has said that sin is separation. Is not segregation an existential expression of man's tragic separation, his awful estrangement, his terrible sinfulness? Thus it is that I can urge men to obey the 1954 decision of the Supreme Court, for it is morally right; and I can urge them to disobey segregation ordinances, for they are morally wrong.

Let us consider a more concrete example of just and unjust laws. An unjust law is a code that a numerical or power majority group compels a minority group to obey but does not make binding on itself. This is difference made legal. By the same token, a just law is a code that a majority compels a minority to follow and that it is willing to follow itself. This is sameness made legal. Let me give another explanation. A law is unjust if it is inflicted on a minority that, as a result of being denied the right to vote, had no part in enacting or devising the law. Who can say that the legislature of Alabama which set up that state's segregation laws was democratically elected? Throughout Alabama all sorts of devious methods are used to prevent Negroes from becoming registered voters, and there are some counties in which, even though Negroes constitute a majority of the population, not a single Negro is registered. Can any law enacted under such circumstances be considered democratically structured?

Sometimes a law is just on its face and unjust in its application. For instance, I have been arrested on a charge of parading without a permit. Now, there is nothing wrong in having an ordinance which requires a permit for a parade. But such an ordinance becomes unjust when it is used to maintain segregation and to deny citizens the First-Amendment privilege of peaceful assembly and protest.

I hope you are able to see the distinction I am trying to point out. In no sense do I advocate evading or defying the law, as would the rabid segregationist. That would lead to anarchy. One who breaks an unjust law must do so openly, lovingly, and with a willingness to accept the penalty. I submit that an individual who breaks a law that conscience tells him is unjust, and who willingly accepts the penalty of imprisonment in order to arouse the conscience of the community over its injustice, is in reality expressing the highest respect for law.

Of course, there is nothing new about this kind of civil disobedience. It was evidenced sublimely in the refusal of Shadrach, Meshach and Abednego to obey the laws of Nebuchadnezzar, on the ground that a higher moral law was at stake. It was practiced superbly by the early Christians, who were willing to face hungry lions and the excruciating pain of chopping blocks rather than submit to certain unjust laws of the Roman Empire. To a degree, academic freedom is a reality today because Socrates practiced civil disobedience. In our own nation, the Boston Tea Party represented a massive act of civil disobedience.

We should never forget that everything Adolf Hitler did in Germany was "legal" and everything the Hungarian freedom fighters did in Hungary was "illegal." It was "illegal" to aid and comfort a Jew in Hitler's Germany. Even so, I am sure that, had I lived in Germany at the time, I would have aided and comforted my Jewish brothers. If today I lived in a Communist country where certain principles dear to the Christian faith are suppressed, I would openly advocate disobeying that country's antireligious laws.

I must make two honest confessions to you, my Christian and Jewish brothers. First, I must confess that over the past few years I have been gravely disappointed with the white moderate. I have almost reached the regrettable conclusion that the Negro's great stumbling block in his stride toward freedom is not the White Citizen's Counciler or the Ku Klux Klanner, but the white moderate, who is more devoted to "order" than to justice; who prefers a negative peace which is the absence of tension to a positive peace which is the presence of justice; who constantly says: "I agree with you in the goal you seek, but I cannot agree with your methods of direct action"; who paternalistically believes he can set the timetable for another man's freedom; who lives by a mythical concept of time and who constantly advises the Negro to wait for a "more convenient season." Shallow understanding from people of good will is more frustrating than absolute misunderstanding from people of ill will. Lukewarm acceptance is much more bewildering than outright rejection.

I had hoped that the white moderate would understand that law and order exist for the purpose of establishing justice and that when they fail in this purpose they become the dangerously structured dams that block the flow of social progress. I had hoped that the white moderate would understand that the present tension in the South is a necessary phase of the transition from an obnoxious negative peace, in which the Negro passively accepted his unjust plight, to a substantive and positive peace, in which all men will respect the dignity and worth of human personality. Actually, we who engage in nonviolent direct action are not the creators of tension. We merely bring to the surface the hidden tension that is already alive. We bring it out in the open, where it can be seen and dealt with. Like a boil that can never be cured so long as it is covered up but must be opened with all its ugliness to the natural medicines of air and light, injustice must be exposed, with all the tension its exposure creates, to the light of human conscience and the air of national opinion before it can be cured.

In your statement you assert that our actions, even though peaceful, must be condemned because they precipitate violence. But is this a logical assertion? Isn't this like condemning a robbed man because his possession of money precipitated the evil act of robbery? Isn't this like condemning Socrates because his unswerving commitment to truth and his philosophical inquiries precipitated the act by the misguided populace in which they made him drink hemlock? Isn't this like condemning Jesus because his unique God consciousness and never ceasing devotion to God's will precipitated the evil act of crucifixion? We must come to see that, as the federal courts have consistently affirmed, it is wrong to urge an individual to cease his efforts to gain his basic constitutional rights because the quest may precipitate violence. Society must protect the robbed and punish the robber. I had also hoped that the white moderate would reject the myth concerning time in relation to the struggle for freedom. I have just received a letter from a white brother in Texas. He writes: "All Christians know that the colored people will receive equal rights eventually, but it is possible that you are in too great a religious hurry. It has taken Christianity almost two thousand years to accomplish what it has. The teachings of Christ take time to come to earth." Such an attitude stems from a tragic misconception of time, from the strangely irrational notion that there is something in the very flow of time that will inevitably cure all ills. Actually, time itself is neutral; it can be used either destructively or constructively. More and more I feel that the people of ill will have used time much more effectively than have the people of good will. We will have to repent in this generation not merely for the hateful words and actions of the bad people but for the appalling silence of the good people. Human progress never rolls in on wheels of inevitability; it comes through the tireless efforts of men willing to be co workers with God, and without this hard work, time itself becomes an ally of the forces of social stagnation. We must use time creatively, in the knowledge that the time is always ripe to do right. Now is the time to make real the promise of democracy and transform our pending national elegy into a creative psalm of brotherhood. Now is the time to lift our national policy from the quicksand of racial injustice to the solid rock of human dignity.

You speak of our activity in Birmingham as extreme. At first I was rather disappointed that fellow clergymen would see my nonviolent efforts as those of an extremist. I began thinking about the fact that I stand in the middle of two opposing forces in the Negro community. One is a force of complacency, made up in part of Negroes who, as a result of long years of oppression, are so drained of self respect and a sense of "somebodiness" that they have adjusted to segregation; and in part of a few middle-class Negroes who, because of a degree of academic and economic security and because in some ways they profit by segregation, have become insensitive to the problems of the masses. The other force is one of bitterness and hatred, and it comes perilously close to advocating violence. It is expressed in the various black nationalist groups that are springing up across the nation, the largest and best known being Elijah Muhammad's Muslim movement. Nourished by the Negro's frustration over the continued existence of racial discrimination, this movement is made up of people who have lost faith in America, who have absolutely repudiated Christianity, and who have concluded that the white man is an incorrigible "devil."

I have tried to stand between these two forces, saying that we need emulate neither the "do nothingism" of the complacent nor the hatred and despair of the black nationalist. For there is the more excellent way of love and nonviolent protest. I am grateful to God that, through the influence of the Negro church, the way of nonviolence became an integral part of our struggle. If this philosophy had not emerged, by now many streets of the South would, I am convinced, be flowing with blood. And I am further convinced that if our white brothers dismiss as "rabble rousers" and "outside agitators" those of us who employ nonviolent direct action, and if they refuse to support our nonviolent efforts, millions of Negroes will, out of frustration and despair, seek solace and security in black nationalist ideologies—a development that would inevitably lead to a frightening racial nightmare.

Oppressed people cannot remain oppressed forever. The yearning for freedom eventually manifests itself, and that is what has happened to the American Negro. Something within has reminded him of his birthright of freedom, and something without has reminded him that it can be gained. Consciously or unconsciously, he has been caught up by the Zeitgeist, and with his black brothers of Africa and his brown and yellow brothers of Asia, South America and the Caribbean, the United States Negro is moving with a sense of great urgency toward the promised land of racial justice. If one recognizes this vital urge that has engulfed the Negro community, one should readily understand why public demonstrations are taking place. The Negro has many pent up resentments and latent frustrations, and he must release them. So let him march; let him make prayer pilgrimages to the city hall; let him go on freedom rides -and try to understand why he must do so. If his repressed emotions are not released in nonviolent ways, they will seek expression through violence; this is not a threat but a fact of history. So I have not said to my people: "Get rid of your discontent." Rather, I have tried to say that this normal and healthy discontent can be channeled into the creative outlet of nonviolent direct action. And now this approach is being termed extremist. But though I was initially disappointed at being categorized as an extremist, as I continued to think about the matter I gradually gained a measure of satisfaction from the label. Was not Jesus an extremist for love: "Love your enemies, bless them that curse you, do good to them that hate you, and pray for them which despitefully use you, and persecute you." Was not Amos an extremist for justice: "Let justice roll down like waters and righteousness like an ever flowing stream." Was not Paul an extremist for the Christian gospel: "I bear in my body the marks of the Lord Jesus." Was not Martin Luther an extremist: "Here I stand; I cannot do otherwise, so help me God." And John Bunyan: "I will stay in jail to the end of my days before I make a butchery of my conscience." And Abraham Lincoln: "This nation cannot survive half slave and half free." And Thomas Jefferson: "We hold these truths to be self evident, that all men are created equal . . ." So the question is not whether we will be extremists, but what kind of extremists we will be. Will we be extremists for hate or for love? Will we be extremists for the preservation of injustice or for the extension of justice? In that dramatic scene on Calvary's hill three men were crucified. We must never forget that all three were crucified for the same crime—the crime of extremism. Two were extremists for immorality, and thus fell below their environment. The other, Jesus Christ, was an extremist for love, truth and goodness, and thereby rose above his environment. Perhaps the South, the nation and the world are in dire need of creative extremists.

I had hoped that the white moderate would see this need. Perhaps I was too optimistic; perhaps I expected too much. I suppose I should have realized that few members of the oppressor race can understand the deep groans and passionate yearnings of the oppressed race, and still fewer have the vision to see that injustice must be rooted out by strong, persistent and determined action. I am thankful, however, that some of our white brothers in the South have grasped the meaning of this social revolution and committed themselves to it. They are still all too few in quantity, but they are big in quality. Some -such as Ralph McGill, Lillian Smith, Harry Golden, James McBride Dabbs, Ann Braden and Sarah Patton Boyle—have written about our struggle in eloquent and prophetic terms. Others have marched with us down nameless streets of the South. They have languished in filthy, roach infested jails, suffering the abuse and brutality of policemen who view them as "dirty nigger-lovers." Unlike so many of their moderate brothers and sisters, they have recognized the urgency of the moment and sensed the need for powerful "action" antidotes to combat the disease of segregation. Let me take note of my other major disappointment. I have been so greatly disappointed with the white church and its leadership. Of course, there are some notable exceptions. I am not unmindful of the fact that each of you has taken some significant stands on this issue. I commend you, Reverend Stallings, for your Christian stand on this past Sunday, in welcoming Negroes to your worship service on a nonsegregated basis. I commend the Catholic leaders of this state for integrating Spring Hill College several years ago.

But despite these notable exceptions, I must honestly reiterate that I have been disappointed with the church. I do not say this as one of those negative critics who can always find something wrong with the church. I say this as a minister of the gospel, who loves the church; who was nurtured in its bosom; who has been sustained by its spiritual blessings and who will remain true to it as long as the cord of life shall lengthen.

When I was suddenly catapulted into the leadership of the bus protest in Montgomery, Alabama, a few years ago, I felt we would be supported by the white church. I felt that the white ministers, priests and rabbis of the South would be among our strongest allies. Instead, some have been outright opponents, refusing to understand the freedom movement and misrepresenting its leaders; all too many others have been more cautious

than courageous and have remained silent behind the anesthe-
tizing security of stained glass windows.

In spite of my shattered dreams, I came to Birmingham with
the hope that the white religious leadership of this community
would see the justice of our cause and, with deep moral concern,
would serve as the channel through which our just grievances
could reach the power structure. I had hoped that each of you
would understand. But again I have been disappointed.

I have heard numerous southern religious leaders admon-
ish their worshipers to comply with a desegregation decision
because it is the law, but I have longed to hear white ministers
declare: "Follow this decree because integration is morally right
and because the Negro is your brother." In the midst of blatant
injustices inflicted upon the Negro, I have watched white
churchmen stand on the sideline and mouth pious irrelevancies
and sanctimonious trivialities. In the midst of a mighty struggle
to rid our nation of racial and economic injustice, I have heard
many ministers say: "Those are social issues, with which the
gospel has no real concern." And I have watched many churches
commit themselves to a completely other worldly religion
which makes a strange, un-Biblical distinction between body
and soul, between the sacred and the secular.

I have traveled the length and breadth of Alabama, Missis-
sippi and all the other southern states. On sweltering summer
days and crisp autumn mornings I have looked at the South's
beautiful churches with their lofty spires pointing heavenward.
I have beheld the impressive outlines of her massive religious
education buildings. Over and over I have found myself asking:
"What kind of people worship here? Who is their God?
Where were their voices when the lips of Governor Barnett
dripped with words of interposition and nullification? Where

were they when Governor Wallace gave a clarion call for defiance and hatred? Where were their voices of support when bruised and weary Negro men and women decided to rise from the dark dungeons of complacency to the bright hills of creative protest?"

Yes, these questions are still in my mind. In deep disappointment I have wept over the laxity of the church. But be assured that my tears have been tears of love. There can be no deep disappointment where there is not deep love. Yes, I love the church. How could I do otherwise? I am in the rather unique position of being the son, the grandson and the great grandson of preachers. Yes, I see the church as the body of Christ. But, oh! How we have blemished and scarred that body through social neglect and through fear of being nonconformists.

There was a time when the church was very powerful—in the time when the early Christians rejoiced at being deemed worthy to suffer for what they believed. In those days the church was not merely a thermometer that recorded the ideas and principles of popular opinion; it was a thermostat that transformed the mores of society. Whenever the early Christians entered a town, the people in power became disturbed and immediately sought to convict the Christians for being "disturbers of the peace" and "outside agitators.'" But the Christians pressed on, in the conviction that they were "a colony of heaven," called to obey God rather than man. Small in number, they were big in commitment. They were too God-intoxicated to be "astronomically intimidated." By their effort and example they brought an end to such ancient evils as infanticide and gladiatorial contests. Things are different now. So often the contemporary church is a weak, ineffectual voice with an uncertain sound. So often it is an archdefender of the status quo. Far from being disturbed by the presence of the church, the power structure of the average community is consoled by the church's silent—and often even vocal—sanction of things as they are.

But the judgment of God is upon the church as never before. If today's church does not recapture the sacrificial spirit of the early church, it will lose its authenticity, forfeit the loyalty of millions, and be dismissed as an irrelevant social club with no meaning for the twentieth century. Every day I meet young people whose disappointment with the church has turned into outright disgust.

Perhaps I have once again been too optimistic. Is organized religion too inextricably bound to the status quo to save our nation and the world? Perhaps I must turn my faith to the inner spiritual church, the church within the church, as the true ekklesia and the hope of the world. But again I am thankful to God that some noble souls from the ranks of organized religion have broken loose from the paralyzing chains of conformity and joined us as active partners in the struggle for freedom. They have left their secure congregations and walked the streets of Albany, Georgia, with us. They have gone down the highways of the South on tortuous rides for freedom. Yes, they have gone to jail with us. Some have been dismissed from their churches, have lost the support of their bishops and fellow ministers. But they have acted in the faith that right defeated is stronger than evil triumphant. Their witness has been the spiritual salt that has preserved the true meaning of the gospel in these troubled times. They have carved a tunnel of hope through the dark mountain of disappointment. I hope the church as a whole will meet the challenge of this decisive hour. But even if the church does not come to the aid of justice, I have no despair about the future. I have no fear about the outcome of our struggle in

Birmingham, even if our motives are at present misunderstood. We will reach the goal of freedom in Birmingham and all over the nation, because the goal of America is freedom. Abused and scorned though we may be, our destiny is tied up with America's destiny. Before the pilgrims landed at Plymouth, we were here. Before the pen of Jefferson etched the majestic words of the Declaration of Independence across the pages of history, we were here. For more than two centuries our forebears labored in this country without wages; they made cotton king; they built the homes of their masters while suffering gross injustice and shameful humiliation -and yet out of a bottomless vitality they continued to thrive and develop. If the inexpressible cruelties of slavery could not stop us, the opposition we now face will surely fail. We will win our freedom because the sacred heritage of our nation and the eternal will of God are embodied in our echoing demands. Before closing I feel impelled to mention one other point in your statement that has troubled me profoundly. You warmly commended the Birmingham police force for keeping "order" and "preventing violence." I doubt that you would have so warmly commended the police force if you had seen its dogs sinking their teeth into unarmed, nonviolent Negroes. I doubt that you would so quickly commend the policemen if you were to observe their ugly and inhumane treatment of Negroes here in the city jail; if you were to watch them push and curse old Negro women and young Negro girls; if you were to see them slap and kick old Negro men and young boys; if you were to observe them, as they did on two occasions, refuse to give us food because we wanted to sing our grace together. I cannot join you in your praise of the Birmingham police department.

It is true that the police have exercised a degree of discipline in handling the demonstrators. In this sense they have conducted themselves rather "nonviolently" in public. But for what purpose? To preserve the evil system of segregation. Over the past few years I have consistently preached that nonviolence demands that the means we use must be as pure as the ends we seek. I have tried to make clear that it is wrong to use immoral means to attain moral ends. But now I must affirm that it is just as wrong, or perhaps even more so, to use moral means to preserve immoral ends. Perhaps Mr. Connor and his policemen have been rather nonviolent in public, as was Chief Pritchett in Albany, Georgia, but they have used the moral means of nonviolence to maintain the immoral end of racial injustice. As T. S. Eliot has said: "The last temptation is the greatest treason: To do the right deed for the wrong reason."

I wish you had commended the Negro sit inners and demonstrators of Birmingham for their sublime courage, their willingness to suffer and their amazing discipline in the midst of great provocation. One day the South will recognize its real heroes. They will be the James Merediths, with the noble sense of purpose that enables them to face jeering and hostile mobs, and with the agonizing loneliness that characterizes the life of the pioneer. They will be old, oppressed, battered Negro women, symbolized in a seventy two year old woman in Montgomery, Alabama, who rose up with a sense of dignity and with her people decided not to ride segregated buses, and who responded with ungrammatical profundity to one who inquired about her weariness: "My feets is tired, but my soul is at rest." They will be the young high school and college students, the young ministers of the gospel and a host of their elders, courageously and nonviolently sitting in at lunch counters and willingly going to jail for conscience' sake. One day the South will know that when these disinherited children of God sat down at lunch counters, they were in reality standing up for what is best in the American dream and for the most sacred values in our Judaeo Christian heritage, thereby bringing our nation back to those great wells of democracy which were dug deep by the founding fathers in their formulation of the Constitution and the Declaration of Independence.

Never before have I written so long a letter. I'm afraid it is much too long to take your precious time. I can assure you that it would have been much shorter if I had been writing from a comfortable desk, but what else can one do when he is alone in a narrow jail cell, other than write long letters, think long thoughts and pray long prayers?

If I have said anything in this letter that overstates the truth and indicates an unreasonable impatience, I beg you to forgive me. If I have said anything that understates the truth and indicates my having a patience that allows me to settle for anything less than brotherhood, I beg God to forgive me.

I hope this letter finds you strong in the faith. I also hope that circumstances will soon make it possible for me to meet each of you, not as an integrationist or a civil-rights leader but as a fellow clergyman and a Christian brother. Let us all hope that the dark clouds of racial prejudice will soon pass away and the deep fog of misunderstanding will be lifted from our fear drenched communities, and in some not too distant tomorrow the radiant stars of love and brotherhood will shine over our great nation with all their scintillating beauty.

Yours for the cause of Peace and Brotherhood, Martin Luther King, Jr.

Published in: King, Martin Luther, Jr.[1]

The Declaration of Independence

In Congress, July 4, 1776.

The unanimous Declaration of the thirteen united States of America, When in the Course of human events, it becomes necessary for one people to dissolve the political bands which have connected them with another, and to assume among the powers of the earth, the separate and equal station to which the Laws of Nature and of Nature>s God entitle them, a decent respect to the opinions of mankind requires that they should declare the causes which impel them to the separation.

We hold these truths to be self-evident, that all men are created equal, that they are endowed by their Creator with certain unalienable Rights, that among these are Life, Liberty and the pursuit of Happiness.—That to secure these rights, Governments are instituted among Men, deriving their just powers from the consent of the governed, —That whenever any Form of Government becomes destructive of these ends, it is the Right of the People to alter or to abolish it, and to institute new Government, laying its foundation on such principles and organizing its powers in such form, as to them shall seem most likely to effect their Safety and Happiness. Prudence, indeed, will dictate that Governments long established should not be changed for light and transient causes; and accordingly all experience hath shewn, that mankind are more disposed to suffer, while evils are sufferable, than to right themselves by abolishing the forms to which they are accustomed. But when a long train of abuses and usurpations, pursuing invariably the same Object evinces a design to reduce them under absolute Despotism, it is their right, it is their duty, to throw off such Government, and to provide new Guards for their future security.—Such has been the patient sufferance of these Colonies; and such is now the necessity which constrains them to alter their former Systems of Government. The history of the present King of Great Britain is a history of repeated injuries and usurpations, all having in direct object the establishment of an absolute Tyranny over these States. To prove this, let Facts be submitted to a candid world.

He has refused his Assent to Laws, the most wholesome and necessary for the public good.

He has forbidden his Governors to pass Laws of immediate and pressing importance, unless suspended in their operation till his Assent should be obtained; and when so suspended, he has utterly neglected to attend to them.

He has refused to pass other Laws for the accommodation of large districts of people, unless those people would relinquish the right of Representation in the Legislature, a right inestimable to them and formidable to tyrants only.

He has called together legislative bodies at places unusual, uncomfortable, and distant from the depository of their public Records, for the sole purpose of fatiguing them into compliance with his measures.

He has dissolved Representative Houses repeatedly, for opposing with manly firmness his invasions on the rights of the people.

He has refused for a long time, after such dissolutions, to cause others to be elected; whereby the Legislative powers, incapable of Annihilation, have returned to the People at large for their exercise; the State remaining in the mean time exposed to all the dangers of invasion from without, and convulsions within.

He has endeavoured to prevent the population of these States; for that purpose obstructing the Laws for Naturalization of Foreigners; refusing to pass others to encourage their migrations hither, and raising the conditions of new Appropriations of Lands.

He has obstructed the Administration of Justice, by refusing his Assent to Laws for establishing Judiciary powers.

He has made Judges dependent on his Will alone, for the tenure of their offices, and the amount and payment of their salaries.

He has erected a multitude of New Offices, and sent hither swarms of Officers to harrass our people, and eat out their substance.

He has kept among us, in times of peace, Standing Armies without the Consent of our legislatures.

He has affected to render the Military independent of and superior to the Civil power.

He has combined with others to subject us to a jurisdiction foreign to our constitution, and unacknowledged by our laws; giving his Assent to their Acts of pretended Legislation:

For Quartering large bodies of armed troops among us:

For protecting them, by a mock Trial, from punishment for any Murders which they should commit on the Inhabitants of these States:

For cutting off our Trade with all parts of the world:

For imposing Taxes on us without our Consent:

For depriving us in many cases, of the benefits of Trial by Jury:

For transporting us beyond Seas to be tried for pretended offences:

For abolishing the free System of English Laws in a neighbouring Province, establishing therein an Arbitrary government, and enlarging its Boundaries so as to render it at once an example and fit instrument for introducing the same absolute rule into these Colonies:

For taking away our Charters, abolishing our most valuable Laws, and altering fundamentally the Forms of our Governments:

For suspending our own Legislatures, and declaring themselves invested with power to legislate for us in all cases whatsoever.

He has abdicated Government here, by declaring us out of his Protection and waging War against us.

He has plundered our seas, ravaged our Coasts, burnt our towns, and destroyed the lives of our people.

He is at this time transporting large Armies of foreign Mercenaries to compleat the works of death, desolation and tyranny, already begun with circumstances of Cruelty & perfidy scarcely paralleled in the most barbarous ages, and totally unworthy the Head of a civilized nation.

He has constrained our fellow Citizens taken Captive on the high Seas to bear Arms against their Country, to become the executioners of their friends and Brethren, or to fall themselves by their Hands.

He has excited domestic insurrections amongst us, and has endeavoured to bring on the inhabitants of our frontiers, the merciless Indian Savages, whose known rule of warfare, is an undistinguished destruction of all ages, sexes and conditions.

In every stage of these Oppressions We have Petitioned for Redress in the most humble terms: Our repeated Petitions have been answered only by repeated injury. A Prince whose character is thus marked by every act which may define a Tyrant, is unfit to be the ruler of a free people.

Nor have We been wanting in attentions to our Brittish brethren. We have warned them from time to time of attempts by their legislature to extend an unwarrantable jurisdiction over us. We have reminded them of the circumstances of our emigration and settlement here. We have appealed to their native justice and magnanimity, and we have conjured them by the ties of our common kindred to disavow these usurpations, which, would inevitably interrupt our connections and correspondence. They too have been deaf to the voice of justice and of consanguinity. We must, therefore, acquiesce in the necessity, which denounces our Separation, and hold them, as we hold the rest of mankind, Enemies in War, in Peace Friends.

We, therefore, the Representatives of the united States of America, in General Congress, Assembled, appealing to the Supreme Judge of the world for the rectitude of our intentions, do, in the Name, and by Authority of the good People of these Colonies, solemnly publish and declare, That these United Colonies are, and of Right ought to be Free and Independent

States; that they are Absolved from all Allegiance to the British Crown, and that all political connection between them and the State of Great Britain, is and ought to be totally dissolved; and that as Free and Independent States, they have full Power to levy War, conclude Peace, contract Alliances, establish Commerce, and to do all other Acts and Things which Independent States may of right do. And for the support of this Declaration, with a firm reliance on the protection of divine Providence, we mutually pledge to each other our Lives, our Fortunes and our sacred Honor.

Georgia

Button Gwinnett
Lyman Hall
George Walton

North Carolina

William Hooper
Joseph Hewes
John Penn

South Carolina

Edward Rutledge
Thomas
Heyward, Jr.
Thomas Lynch, Jr.
Arthur Middleton

Massachusetts

John Hancock

Maryland

Samuel Chase
William Paca
Thomas Stone
Charles Carroll
of Carrollton

Virginia

George Wythe
Richard Henry Lee
Thomas Jefferson
Benjamin Harrison
Thomas Nelson, Jr.
Francis Light-
foot Lee
Carter Braxton

Pennsylvania

Robert Morris
Benjamin Rush
Benjamin Franklin
John Morton
George Clymer
James Smith
George Taylor
James Wilson
George Ross

Delaware

Caesar Rodney
George Read
Thomas McKean

New York

William Floyd
Philip Livingston
Francis Lewis
Lewis Morris

New Jersey

Richard Stockton
John Witherspoon
Francis Hopkinson
John Hart
Abraham Clark

New Hampshire

Josiah Bartlett
William Whipple
Matthew Thornton

Massachusetts

Samuel Adams
John Adams
Robert Treat Paine
Elbridge Gerry

Rhode Island

Stephen Hopkins
William Ellery

Connecticut

Roger Sherman
Samuel Huntington
William Williams
Oliver Wolcott

The Constitution of the United States of America

(Note that the italicized words in the Constitution were later amended or suspended.)

W**e the People** of the United States, in Order to form a more perfect Union, establish Justice, insure domestic Tranquility, provide for the common defence, promote the general Welfare, and secure the Blessings of Liberty to ourselves and our Posterity, do ordain and establish this Constitution for the United States of America.

Article. I.

Section. 1.

All legislative Powers herein granted shall be vested in a Congress of the United States, which shall consist of a Senate and House of Representatives.

Section. 2.

The House of Representatives shall be composed of Members chosen every second Year by the People of the several States, and the Electors in each State shall have the Qualifications requisite for Electors of the most numerous Branch of the State Legislature.

No Person shall be a Representative who shall not have attained to the Age of twenty five Years, and been seven Years a

Citizen of the United States, and who shall not, when elected, be an Inhabitant of that State in which he shall be chosen.

Representatives and direct Taxes shall be apportioned among the several States which may be included within this Union, according to their respective Numbers, which shall be determined by adding to the whole Number of free Persons, including those bound to Service for a Term of Years, and excluding Indians not taxed, three fifths of all other Persons. The actual Enumeration shall be made within three Years after the first Meeting of the Congress of the United States, and within every subsequent Term of ten Years, in such Manner as they shall by Law direct. The Number of Representatives shall not exceed one for every thirty Thousand, but each State shall have at Least one Representative; and until such enumeration shall be made, the State of New Hampshire shall be entitled to chuse three, Massachusetts eight, Rhode-Island and Providence Plantations one, Connecticut five, New-York six, New Jersey four, Pennsylvania eight, Delaware one, Maryland six, Virginia ten, North Carolina five, South Carolina five, and Georgia three.

When vacancies happen in the Representation from any State, the Executive Authority thereof shall issue Writs of Election to fill such Vacancies.

The House of Representatives shall chuse their Speaker and other Officers; and shall have the sole Power of Impeachment.

Section. 3.

The Senate of the United States shall be composed of two Senators from each State, *chosen by the Legislature* thereof, for six Years; and each Senator shall have one Vote.

Immediately after they shall be assembled in Consequence

of the first Election, they shall be divided as equally as may be into three Classes. The Seats of the Senators of the first Class shall be vacated at the Expiration of the second Year, of the second Class at the Expiration of the fourth Year, and of the third Class at the Expiration of the sixth Year, so that one third may be chosen every second Year; *and if Vacancies happen by Resignation, or otherwise, during the Recess of the Legislature of any State, the Executive thereof may make temporary Appointments until the next Meeting of the Legislature, which shall then fill such Vacancies.*

No Person shall be a Senator who shall not have attained to the Age of thirty Years, and been nine Years a Citizen of the United States, and who shall not, when elected, be an Inhabitant of that State for which he shall be chosen.

The Vice President of the United States shall be President of the Senate, but shall have no Vote, unless they be equally divided.

The Senate shall chuse their other Officers, and also a President pro tempore, in the Absence of the Vice President, or when he shall exercise the Office of President of the United States.

The Senate shall have the sole Power to try all Impeachments. When sitting for that Purpose, they shall be on Oath or Affirmation. When the President of the United States is tried, the Chief Justice shall preside: And no Person shall be convicted without the Concurrence of two thirds of the Members present.

Judgment in Cases of Impeachment shall not extend further than to removal from Office, and disqualification to hold and enjoy any Office of honor, Trust or Profit under the United States: but the Party convicted shall nevertheless be liable and subject to Indictment, Trial, Judgment and Punishment, according to Law.

Section. 4.

The Times, Places and Manner of holding Elections for Senators and Representatives, shall be prescribed in each State by the Legislature thereof; but the Congress may at any time by Law make or alter such Regulations, except as to the Places of chusing Senators.

The Congress shall assemble at least once in every Year, and such Meeting shall be on *the first Monday in December*, unless they shall by Law appoint a different Day.

Section. 5.

Each House shall be the Judge of the Elections, Returns and Qualifications of its own Members, and a Majority of each shall constitute a Quorum to do Business; but a smaller Number may adjourn from day to day, and may be authorized to compel the Attendance of absent Members, in such Manner, and under such Penalties as each House may provide.

Each House may determine the Rules of its Proceedings, punish its Members for disorderly Behaviour, and, with the Concurrence of two thirds, expel a Member.

Each House shall keep a Journal of its Proceedings, and from time to time publish the same, excepting such Parts as may in their Judgment require Secrecy; and the Yeas and Nays of the Members of either House on any question shall, at the Desire of one fifth of those Present, be entered on the Journal.

Neither House, during the Session of Congress, shall, without the Consent of the other, adjourn for more than three days, nor to any other Place than that in which the two Houses shall be sitting.

Section. 6.

The Senators and Representatives shall receive a Compensation for their Services, to be ascertained by Law, and paid out of the Treasury of the United States. They shall in all Cases, except Treason, Felony and Breach of the Peace, be privileged from Arrest during their Attendance at the Session of their respective Houses, and in going to and returning from the same; and for any Speech or Debate in either House, they shall not be questioned in any other Place.

No Senator or Representative shall, during the Time for which he was elected, be appointed to any civil Office under the Authority of the United States, which shall have been created, or the Emoluments whereof shall have been encreased during such time; and no Person holding any Office under the United States, shall be a Member of either House during his Continuance in Office.

Section. 7.

All Bills for raising Revenue shall originate in the House of Representatives; but the Senate may propose or concur with Amendments as on other Bills.

Every Bill which shall have passed the House of Representatives and the Senate, shall, before it become a Law, be presented to the President of the United States; If he approve he shall sign it, but if not he shall return it, with his Objections to that House in which it shall have originated, who shall enter the Objections at large on their Journal, and proceed to reconsider it. If after such Reconsideration two thirds of that House shall agree to pass the Bill, it shall be sent, together with the Objections, to the other House, by which it shall likewise be reconsidered, and if approved by two thirds of that House, it shall become a Law. But in all such Cases the Votes of both Houses shall be determined by yeas and Nays, and the Names of the Persons voting for and against the Bill shall be entered on the Journal of each House respectively. If any Bill shall not be returned by the President within ten Days (Sundays excepted) after it shall have been presented to him, the Same shall be a Law, in like Manner as if he had signed it, unless the Congress by their Adjournment prevent its Return, in which Case it shall not be a Law.

Every Order, Resolution, or Vote to which the Concurrence of the Senate and House of Representatives may be necessary (except on a question of Adjournment) shall be presented to the President of the United States; and before the Same shall take Effect, shall be approved by him, or being disapproved by him, shall be repassed by two thirds of the Senate and House of Representatives, according to the Rules and Limitations prescribed in the Case of a Bill.

Section. 8.

The Congress shall have Power To lay and collect Taxes, Duties, Imposts and Excises, to pay the Debts and provide for the common Defence and general Welfare of the United States; but all Duties, Imposts and Excises shall be uniform throughout the United States;

To borrow Money on the credit of the United States;

To regulate Commerce with foreign Nations, and among the several States, and with the Indian Tribes;

To establish an uniform Rule of Naturalization, and uniform Laws on the subject of Bankruptcies throughout the United States;

To coin Money, regulate the Value thereof, and of foreign Coin, and fix the Standard of Weights and Measures;

To provide for the Punishment of counterfeiting the Securities and current Coin of the United States;

To establish Post Offices and post Roads;

To promote the Progress of Science and useful Arts, by securing for limited Times to Authors and Inventors the exclusive Right to their respective Writings and Discoveries;

To constitute Tribunals inferior to the supreme Court;

To define and punish Piracies and Felonies committed on the high Seas, and Offences against the Law of Nations;

To declare War, grant Letters of Marque and Reprisal, and make Rules concerning Captures on Land and Water;

To raise and support Armies, but no Appropriation of Money to that Use shall be for a longer Term than two Years;

To provide and maintain a Navy; To make Rules for the Government and Regulation of the land and naval Forces;

To provide for calling forth the Militia to execute the Laws of the Union, suppress Insurrections and repel Invasions;

To provide for organizing, arming, and disciplining, the Militia, and for governing such Part of them as may be employed in the Service of the United States, reserving to the States respectively, the Appointment of the Officers, and the Authority of training the Militia according to the discipline prescribed by Congress;

To exercise exclusive Legislation in all Cases whatsoever, over such District (not exceeding ten Miles square) as may, by Cession of particular States, and the Acceptance of Congress, become the Seat of the Government of the United States, and to exercise like Authority over all Places purchased by the Consent of the Legislature of the State in which the Same shall be, for the Erection of Forts, Magazines, Arsenals, dock-Yards, and other needful Buildings;—And

To make all Laws which shall be necessary and proper for carrying into Execution the foregoing Powers, and all other Powers vested by this Constitution in the Government of the United States, or in any Department or Officer thereof.

Section. 9.

The Migration or Importation of such Persons as any of the States now existing shall think proper to admit, shall not be prohibited by the Congress prior to the Year one thousand eight hundred and eight, but a Tax or duty may be imposed on such Importation, not exceeding ten dollars for each Person.

The Privilege of the Writ of Habeas Corpus shall not be suspended, unless when in Cases of Rebellion or Invasion the public Safety may require it.

No Bill of Attainder or ex post facto Law shall be passed.

No Capitation, or other direct, Tax shall be laid, *unless in Proportion to the Census or enumeration herein before directed to be taken.*

No Tax or Duty shall be laid on Articles exported from any State.

No Preference shall be given by any Regulation of Commerce or Revenue to the Ports of one State over those of another: nor shall Vessels bound to, or from, one State, be obliged to enter, clear, or pay Duties in another.

No Money shall be drawn from the Treasury, but in Consequence of Appropriations made by Law; and a regular Statement and Account of the Receipts and Expenditures of all public Money shall be published from time to time.

No Title of Nobility shall be granted by the United States: And no Person holding any Office of Profit or Trust under them, shall, without the Consent of the Congress, accept of any present, Emolument, Office, or Title, of any kind whatever, from any King, Prince, or foreign State.

Section. 10.

No State shall enter into any Treaty, Alliance, or Confederation; grant Letters of Marque and Reprisal; coin Money; emit Bills of Credit; make any Thing but gold and silver Coin a Tender in Payment of Debts; pass any Bill of Attainder, ex post facto Law, or Law impairing the Obligation of Contracts, or grant any Title of Nobility.

No State shall, without the Consent of the Congress, lay any Imposts or Duties on Imports or Exports, except what may be absolutely necessary for executing it's inspection Laws: and the net Produce of all Duties and Imposts, laid by any State on Imports or Exports, shall be for the Use of the Treasury of the United States; and all such Laws shall be subject to the Revision and Controul of the Congress.

No State shall, without the Consent of Congress, lay any Duty of Tonnage, keep Troops, or Ships of War in time of Peace, enter into any Agreement or Compact with another State, or with a foreign Power, or engage in War, unless actually invaded, or in such imminent Danger as will not admit of delay.

ARTICLE. II.

Section. 1.

The executive Power shall be vested in a President of the United States of America. He shall hold his Office during the Term of four Years, and, together with the Vice President, chosen for the same Term, be elected, as follows:

Each State shall appoint, in such Manner as the Legislature

thereof may direct, a Number of Electors, equal to the whole Number of Senators and Representatives to which the State may be entitled in the Congress: but no Senator or Representative, or Person holding an Office of Trust or Profit under the United States, shall be appointed an Elector.

The Electors shall meet in their respective States, and vote by Ballot for two Persons, of whom one at least shall not be an Inhabitant of the same State with themselves. And they shall make a List of all the Persons voted for, and of the Number of Votes for each; which List they shall sign and certify, and transmit sealed to the Seat of the Government of the United States, directed to the President of the Senate. The President of the Senate shall, in the Presence of the Senate and House of Representatives, open all the Certificates, and the Votes shall then be counted. The Person having the greatest Number of Votes shall be the President, if such Number be a Majority of the whole Number of Electors appointed; and if there be more than one who have such Majority, and have an equal Number of Votes, then the House of Representatives shall immediately chuse by Ballot one of them for President; and if no Person have a Majority, then from the five highest on the List the said House shall in like Manner chuse the President. But in chusing the President, the Votes shall be taken by States, the Representation from each State having one Vote; A quorum for this Purpose shall consist of a Member or Members from two thirds of the States, and a Majority of all the States shall be necessary to a Choice. In every Case, after the Choice of the President, the Person having the greatest Number of Votes of the Electors shall be the Vice President. But if there should remain two or more who have equal Votes, the Senate shall chuse from them by Ballot the Vice President.

The Congress may determine the Time of chusing the

Electors, and the Day on which they shall give their Votes; which Day shall be the same throughout the United States.

No Person except a natural born Citizen, or a Citizen of the United States, at the time of the Adoption of this Constitution, shall be eligible to the Office of President; neither shall any Person be eligible to that Office who shall not have attained to the Age of thirty five Years, and been fourteen Years a Resident within the United States.

In Case of the Removal of the President from Office, or of his Death, Resignation, or Inability to discharge the Powers and Duties of the said Office, the Same shall devolve on the Vice President, and the Congress may by Law provide for the Case of Removal, Death, Resignation or Inability, both of the President and Vice President, declaring what Officer shall then act as President, and such Officer shall act accordingly, until the Disability be removed, or a President shall be elected.

The President shall, at stated Times, receive for his Services, a Compensation, which shall neither be encreased nor diminished during the Period for which he shall have been elected, and he shall not receive within that Period any other Emolument from the United States, or any of them.

Before he enter on the Execution of his Office, he shall take the following Oath or Affirmation:—"I do solemnly swear (or affirm) that I will faithfully execute the Office of President of the United States, and will to the best of my Ability, preserve, protect and defend the Constitution of the United States."

Section. 2.

The President shall be Commander in Chief of the Army and Navy of the United States, and of the Militia of the several States, when called into the actual Service of the United States;

he may require the Opinion, in writing, of the principal Officer in each of the executive Departments, upon any Subject relating to the Duties of their respective Offices, and he shall have Power to grant Reprieves and Pardons for Offences against the United States, except in Cases of Impeachment.

He shall have Power, by and with the Advice and Consent of the Senate, to make Treaties, provided two thirds of the Senators present concur; and he shall nominate, and by and with the Advice and Consent of the Senate, shall appoint Ambassadors, other public Ministers and Consuls, Judges of the supreme Court, and all other Officers of the United States, whose Appointments are not herein otherwise provided for, and which shall be established by Law: but the Congress may by Law vest the Appointment of such inferior Officers, as they think proper, in the President alone, in the Courts of Law, or in the Heads of Departments.

The President shall have Power to fill up all Vacancies that may happen during the Recess of the Senate, by granting Commissions which shall expire at the End of their next Session.

Section. 3.

He shall from time to time give to the Congress Information of the State of the Union, and recommend to their Consideration such Measures as he shall judge necessary and expedient; he may, on extraordinary Occasions, convene both Houses, or either of them, and in Case of Disagreement between them, with Respect to the Time of Adjournment, he may adjourn them to such Time as he shall think proper; he shall receive Ambassadors and other public Ministers; he shall take Care that the Laws be faithfully executed, and shall Commission all the Officers of the United States.

Section. 4.

The President, Vice President and all civil Officers of the United States, shall be removed from Office on Impeachment for, and Conviction of, Treason, Bribery, or other high Crimes and Misdemeanors.

ARTICLE III.

Section. 1.

The judicial Power of the United States, shall be vested in one supreme Court, and in such inferior Courts as the Congress may from time to time ordain and establish. The Judges, both of the supreme and inferior Courts, shall hold their Offices during good Behaviour, and shall, at stated Times, receive for their Services, a Compensation, which shall not be diminished during their Continuance in Office.

Section. 2.

The judicial Power shall extend to all Cases, in Law and Equity, arising under this Constitution, the Laws of the United States, and Treaties made, or which shall be made, under their Authority;—to all Cases affecting Ambassadors, other public Ministers and Consuls;—to all Cases of admiralty and maritime Jurisdiction;—to Controversies to which the United States shall be a Party;—to Controversies between two or more States;—*between a State and Citizens of another State,*—between Citizens of different States,—between Citizens of the same State claiming Lands under Grants of different States, *and between a State, or the Citizens thereof, and foreign States, Citizens or Subjects.*

In all Cases affecting Ambassadors, other public Ministers and Consuls, and those in which a State shall be Party, the supreme Court shall have original Jurisdiction. In all the other Cases before mentioned, the supreme Court shall have appellate Jurisdiction, both as to Law and Fact, with such Exceptions, and under such Regulations as the Congress shall make.

The Trial of all Crimes, except in Cases of Impeachment, shall be by Jury; and such Trial shall be held in the State where the said Crimes shall have been committed; but when not committed within any State, the Trial shall be at such Place or Places as the Congress may by Law have directed.

Section. 3.

Treason against the United States, shall consist only in levying War against them, or in adhering to their Enemies, giving them Aid and Comfort. No Person shall be convicted of Treason unless on the Testimony of two Witnesses to the same overt Act, or on Confession in open Court.

The Congress shall have Power to declare the Punishment of Treason, but no Attainder of Treason shall work Corruption of Blood, or Forfeiture except during the Life of the Person attainted.

Article. IV.

Section. 1.

Full Faith and Credit shall be given in each State to the public Acts, Records, and judicial Proceedings of every other State. And the Congress may by general Laws prescribe the Manner in which such Acts, Records and Proceedings shall be proved, and the Effect thereof.

Section. 2.

The Citizens of each State shall be entitled to all Privileges and Immunities of Citizens in the several States.

A Person charged in any State with Treason, Felony, or other Crime, who shall flee from Justice, and be found in another State, shall on Demand of the executive Authority of the State from which he fled, be delivered up, to be removed to the State having Jurisdiction of the Crime.

No Person held to Service or Labour in one State, under the Laws thereof, escaping into another, shall, in Consequence of any Law or Regulation therein, be discharged from such Service or Labour, but shall be delivered up on Claim of the Party to whom such Service or Labour may be due.

Section. 3.

New States may be admitted by the Congress into this Union; but no new State shall be formed or erected within the Jurisdiction of any other State; nor any State be formed by the Junction of two or more States, or Parts of States, without the Consent of the Legislatures of the States concerned as well as of the Congress.

The Congress shall have Power to dispose of and make all needful Rules and Regulations respecting the Territory or other Property belonging to the United States; and nothing in this Constitution shall be so construed as to Prejudice any Claims of the United States, or of any particular State.

Section. 4.

The United States shall guarantee to every State in this Union a Republican Form of Government, and shall protect each of them against Invasion; and on Application of the Legislature, or of the Executive (when the Legislature cannot be convened), against domestic Violence.

Article. V.

The Congress, whenever two thirds of both Houses shall deem it necessary, shall propose Amendments to this Constitution, or, on the Application of the Legislatures of two thirds of the several States, shall call a Convention for proposing Amendments, which, in either Case, shall be valid to all Intents and Purposes, as Part of this Constitution, when ratified by the Legislatures of three fourths of the several States, or by Conventions in three fourths thereof, as the one or the other Mode of Ratification may be proposed by the Congress; Provided that no Amendment which may be made prior to the Year One thousand eight hundred and eight shall in any Manner affect the first and fourth Clauses in the Ninth Section of the first Article; and that no State, without its Consent, shall be deprived of its equal Suffrage in the Senate.

Article. VI.

All Debts contracted and Engagements entered into, before the Adoption of this Constitution, shall be as valid against the United States under this Constitution, as under the Confederation.

This Constitution, and the Laws of the United States which shall be made in Pursuance thereof; and all Treaties made, or which shall be made, under the Authority of the United States, shall be the supreme Law of the Land; and the Judges in every

State shall be bound thereby, any Thing in the Constitution or Laws of any State to the Contrary notwithstanding.

The Senators and Representatives before mentioned, and the Members of the several State Legislatures, and all executive and judicial Officers, both of the United States and of the several States, shall be bound by Oath or Affirmation, to support this Constitution; but no religious Test shall ever be required as a Qualification to any Office or public Trust under the United States.

ARTICLE. VII.

The Ratification of the Conventions of nine States, shall be sufficient for the Establishment of this Constitution between the States so ratifying the Same.

Done in Convention by the Unanimous Consent of the States present the Seventeenth Day of September in the Year of our Lord one thousand seven hundred and Eighty seven and of the Independance of the United States of America the Twelfth In witness whereof We have hereunto subscribed our Names,

G°. Washington—Presidt. and deputy from Virginia

Delaware

Geo: Read
Gunning
Bedford jun
John Dickinson
Richard Bassett
Jaco: Broom

Maryland

James McHenry
Dan of St
Thos. Jenifer
Danl. Carroll

Virginia

John Blair
James Madison Jr.

North Carolina

Wm. Blount
Richd.
Dobbs Spaight
Hu Williamson

South Carolina

J. Rutledge
Charles Cotes-
worth Pinckney
Charles Pinckney
Pierce Butler

Georgia

William Few
Abr Baldwin

New Hampshire

John Langdon
Nicholas Gilman

Massachusetts

Nathaniel Gorham
Rufus King

Connecticut

Wm. Saml. Johnson
Roger Sherman

New York

Alexander Hamilton

New Jersey

Wil: Livingston
David Brearley
Wm. Paterson
Jona: Dayton

Pennsylvania

B Franklin
Thomas Mifflin
Robt. Morris
Geo. Clymer
Thos. FitzSimons
Jared Ingersoll
James Wilson
Gouv Morris

Amendments to the Constitution of the United States of America

(The first ten amendments, also known as the Bill of Rights, were ratified on December 15, 1791.)

Amendment I

Congress shall make no law respecting an establishment of religion, or prohibiting the free exercise thereof; or abridging the freedom of speech, or of the press; or the right of the people peaceably to assemble, and to petition the Government for a redress of grievances.

Amendment II

A well regulated Militia, being necessary to the security of a free State, the right of the people to keep and bear Arms, shall not be infringed.

Amendment III

No Soldier shall, in time of peace be quartered in any house, without the consent of the Owner, nor in time of war, but in a manner to be prescribed by law.

Amendment IV

The right of the people to be secure in their persons, houses, papers, and effects, against unreasonable searches and seizures, shall not be violated, and no Warrants shall issue, but upon probable cause, supported by Oath or affirmation, and particularly describing the place to be searched, and the persons or things to be seized.

Amendment V

No person shall be held to answer for a capital, or otherwise infamous crime, unless on a presentment or indictment of a Grand Jury, except in cases arising in the land or naval forces, or in the Militia, when in actual service in time of War or public danger; nor shall any person be subject for the same offence to be twice put in jeopardy of life or limb; nor shall be compelled in any criminal case to be a witness against himself, nor be deprived of life, liberty, or property, without due process of law; nor shall private property be taken for public use, without just compensation.

Amendment VI

In all criminal prosecutions, the accused shall enjoy the right to a speedy and public trial, by an impartial jury of the State and district wherein the crime shall have been committed, which district shall have been previously ascertained by law, and to be informed of the nature and cause of the accusation; to be confronted with the witnesses against him; to have compulsory process for obtaining witnesses in his favor, and to have the Assistance of Counsel for his defence.

Amendment VII

In Suits at common law, where the value in controversy shall exceed twenty dollars, the right of trial by jury shall be preserved, and no fact tried by a jury, shall be otherwise re-examined in any Court of the United States, than according to the rules of the common law.

AMENDMENT VIII

Excessive bail shall not be required, nor excessive fines imposed, nor cruel and unusual punishments inflicted.

AMENDMENT IX

The enumeration in the Constitution, of certain rights, shall not be construed to deny or disparage others retained by the people.

AMENDMENT X

The powers not delegated to the United States by the Constitution, nor prohibited by it to the States, are reserved to the States respectively, or to the people.

AMENDMENT XI

Passed by Congress March 4, 1794. Ratified February 7, 1795.
Note: Article III, section 2, of the Constitution
was modified by amendment 11.

The Judicial power of the United States shall not be construed to extend to any suit in law or equity, commenced or prosecuted against one of the United States by Citizens of another State, or by Citizens or Subjects of any Foreign State.

AMENDMENT XII

Passed by Congress December 9, 1803. Ratified June 15, 1804.
Note: A portion of Article II, section 1 of the Constitution
was superseded by the 12th amendment.

The Electors shall meet in their respective states and vote by ballot for President and Vice-President, one of whom, at least, shall not be an inhabitant of the same state with themselves; they shall name in their ballots the person voted for as President, and in distinct ballots the person voted for as Vice-President, and they shall make distinct lists of all persons voted for as President, and of all persons voted for as Vice-President, and of the number of votes for each, which lists they shall sign and certify, and transmit sealed to the seat of the government of the United States, directed to the President of the Senate; — the President of the Senate shall, in the presence of the Senate and House of Representatives, open all the certificates and the votes shall then be counted;

The person having the greatest number of votes for President, shall be the President, if such number be a majority of the whole number of Electors appointed; and if no person have such majority, then from the persons having the highest numbers not exceeding three on the list of those voted for as President, the House of Representatives shall choose immediately, by ballot, the President. But in choosing the President, the votes shall be taken by states, the representation from each state having one vote; a quorum for this purpose shall consist of a member or members from two-thirds of the states, and a majority of all the states shall be necessary to a choice. And if the House of Representatives shall not choose a President whenever the right of choice shall devolve upon them, before the fourth day of March next following, then the Vice-President shall act as President, as in case of the death or other constitutional disability of the President.

The person having the greatest number of votes as Vice-President, shall be the Vice-President, if such number be a majority of the whole number of Electors appointed, and if no person have a majority, then from the two highest numbers on the list, the Senate shall choose the Vice-President; a quorum for the purpose shall consist of two-thirds of the whole number of Senators, and a majority of the whole number shall be necessary to a choice. But no person constitutionally ineligible to the office of President shall be eligible to that of Vice-President of the United States.

AMENDMENT XIII

Passed by Congress January 31, 1865.
Ratified December 6, 1865.
Note: A portion of Article IV, section 2, of the
Constitution was superseded by the 13th amendment.

Section 1.

Neither slavery nor involuntary servitude, except as a punishment for crime whereof the party shall have been duly convicted, shall exist within the United States, or any place subject to their jurisdiction.

Section 2.

Congress shall have power to enforce this article by appropriate legislation.

AMENDMENT XIV

Passed by Congress June 13, 1866. Ratified July 9, 1868.
Note: Article I, section 2, of the Constitution was modified by
section 2 of the 14th amendment.

Section 1.

All persons born or naturalized in the United States, and
subject to the jurisdiction thereof, are citizens of the United
States and of the State wherein they reside. No State shall make
or enforce any law which shall abridge the privileges or immunities of citizens of the United States; nor shall any State deprive
any person of life, liberty, or property, without due process of
law; nor deny to any person within its jurisdiction the equal
protection of the laws.

Section 2.

Representatives shall be apportioned among the several
States according to their respective numbers, counting the
whole number of persons in each State, excluding Indians not
taxed. But when the right to vote at any election for the choice
of electors for President and Vice-President of the United
States, Representatives in Congress, the Executive and Judicial
officers of a State, or the members of the Legislature thereof,
is denied to any of the male inhabitants of such State, being
twenty-one years of age, and citizens of the United States, or
in any way abridged, except for participation in rebellion, or
other crime, the basis of representation therein shall be reduced
in the proportion which the number of such male citizens shall
bear to the whole number of male citizens twenty-one years of
age in such State.

Section 3.

No person shall be a Senator or Representative in Congress, or elector of President and Vice-President, or hold any office, civil or military, under the United States, or under any State, who, having previously taken an oath, as a member of Congress, or as an officer of the United States, or as a member of any State legislature, or as an executive or judicial officer of any State, to support the Constitution of the United States, shall have engaged in insurrection or rebellion against the same, or given aid or comfort to the enemies thereof. But Congress may by a vote of two-thirds of each House, remove such disability.

Section 4.

The validity of the public debt of the United States, authorized by law, including debts incurred for payment of pensions and bounties for services in suppressing insurrection or rebellion, shall not be questioned. But neither the United States nor any State shall assume or pay any debt or obligation incurred in aid of insurrection or rebellion against the United States, or any claim for the loss or emancipation of any slave; but all such debts, obligations and claims shall be held illegal and void.

Section 5.

The Congress shall have the power to enforce, by appropriate legislation, the provisions of this article.

AMENDMENT XV

Passed by Congress February 26, 1869.
Ratified February 3, 1870.

Section 1.

The right of citizens of the United States to vote shall not be denied or abridged by the United States or by any State on account of race, color, or previous condition of servitude.

Section 2.

The Congress shall have the power to enforce this article by appropriate legislation.

AMENDMENT XVI

Passed by Congress July 2, 1909. Ratified February 3, 1913.
Note: Article I, section 9, of the Constitution was modified by amendment 16.

The Congress shall have power to lay and collect taxes on incomes, from whatever source derived, without apportionment among the several States, and without regard to any census or enumeration.

AMENDMENT XVII

Passed by Congress May 13, 1912. Ratified April 8, 1913.
Note: Article I, section 3, of the Constitution was modified by the 17th amendment.

The Senate of the United States shall be composed of two Senators from each State, elected by the people thereof, for six years; and each Senator shall have one vote. The electors in each State shall have the qualifications requisite for electors of the most numerous branch of the State legislatures.

When vacancies happen in the representation of any State

in the Senate, the executive authority of such State shall issue writs of election to fill such vacancies: Provided, That the legislature of any State may empower the executive thereof to make temporary appointments until the people fill the vacancies by election as the legislature may direct.

This amendment shall not be so construed as to affect the election or term of any Senator chosen before it becomes valid as part of the Constitution.

AMENDMENT XVIII

Passed by Congress December 18, 1917.
Ratified January 16, 1919. Repealed by amendment 21.

Section 1.

After one year from the ratification of this article the manufacture, sale, or transportation of intoxicating liquors within, the importation thereof into, or the exportation thereof from the United States and all territory subject to the jurisdiction thereof for beverage purposes is hereby prohibited.

Section 2.

The Congress and the several States shall have concurrent power to enforce this article by appropriate legislation.

Section 3.

This article shall be inoperative unless it shall have been ratified as an amendment to the Constitution by the legislatures of the several States, as provided in the Constitution, within seven years from the date of the submission hereof to the States by the Congress.

AMENDMENT XIX

Passed by Congress June 4, 1919. Ratified August 18, 1920.

The right of citizens of the United States to vote shall not be denied or abridged by the United States or by any State on account of sex.

Congress shall have power to enforce this article by appropriate legislation.

AMENDMENT XX

Passed by Congress March 2, 1932. Ratified January 23, 1933.
Note: Article I, section 4, of the Constitution was modified by section 2 of this amendment. In addition, a portion of the 12th amendment was superseded by section 3.

Section 1.

The terms of the President and the Vice President shall end at noon on the 20th day of January, and the terms of Senators and Representatives at noon on the 3d day of January, of the years in which such terms would have ended if this article had not been ratified; and the terms of their successors shall then begin.

Section 2.

The Congress shall assemble at least once in every year, and such meeting shall begin at noon on the 3d day of January, unless they shall by law appoint a different day.

Section 3.

If, at the time fixed for the beginning of the term of the

President, the President elect shall have died, the Vice President elect shall become President. If a President shall not have been chosen before the time fixed for the beginning of his term, or if the President elect shall have failed to qualify, then the Vice President elect shall act as President until a President shall have qualified; and the Congress may by law provide for the case wherein neither a President elect nor a Vice President elect shall have qualified, declaring who shall then act as President, or the manner in which one who is to act shall be selected, and such person shall act accordingly until a President or Vice President shall have qualified.

Section 4.

The Congress may by law provide for the case of the death of any of the persons from whom the House of Representatives may choose a President whenever the right of choice shall have devolved upon them, and for the case of the death of any of the persons from whom the Senate may choose a Vice President whenever the right of choice shall have devolved upon them.

Section 5.

Sections 1 and 2 shall take effect on the 15th day of October following the ratification of this article.

Section 6.

This article shall be inoperative unless it shall have been ratified as an amendment to the Constitution by the legislatures of three-fourths of the several States within seven years from the date of its submission.

AMENDMENT XXI

Passed by Congress February 20, 1933.
Ratified December 5, 1933.

Section 1.

The eighteenth article of amendment to the Constitution of the United States is hereby repealed.

Section 2.

The transportation or importation into any State, Territory, or possession of the United States for delivery or use therein of intoxicating liquors, in violation of the laws thereof, is hereby prohibited.

Section 3.

This article shall be inoperative unless it shall have been ratified as an amendment to the Constitution by conventions in the several States, as provided in the Constitution, within seven years from the date of the submission hereof to the States by the Congress.

AMENDMENT XXII

Passed by Congress March 21, 1947.
Ratified February 27, 1951.

Section 1.

No person shall be elected to the office of the President more than twice, and no person who has held the office of President, or acted as President, for more than two years of a term to which some other person was elected President shall be elected to the office of the President more than once. But this Article shall not apply to any person holding the office of President when this Article was proposed by the Congress, and shall not prevent any person who may be holding the office of President, or acting as President, during the term within which this Article becomes operative from holding the office of President or acting as President during the remainder of such term.

Section 2.

This article shall be inoperative unless it shall have been ratified as an amendment to the Constitution by the legislatures of three-fourths of the several States within seven years from the date of its submission to the States by the Congress.

AMENDMENT XXIII

Passed by Congress June 16, 1960. Ratified March 29, 1961.

Section 1.

The District constituting the seat of Government of the United States shall appoint in such manner as the Congress may direct: A number of electors of President and Vice President equal to the whole number of Senators and Representatives in Congress to which the District would be entitled if it were a State, but in no event more than the least populous State; they shall be in addition to those appointed by the States, but they shall be considered, for the purposes of the election of President and Vice President, to be electors appointed by a State; and they shall meet in the District and perform such duties as provided by the twelfth article of amendment.

Section 2.

The Congress shall have power to enforce this article by appropriate legislation.

AMENDMENT XXIV

Passed by Congress August 27, 1962. Ratified January 23, 1964.

Section 1.

The right of citizens of the United States to vote in any primary or other election for President or Vice President, for electors for President or Vice President, or for Senator or Representative in Congress, shall not be denied or abridged by the United States or any State by reason of failure to pay any poll tax or other tax.

Section 2.

The Congress shall have power to enforce this article by appropriate legislation.

AMENDMENT XXV

Passed by Congress July 6, 1965. Ratified February 10, 1967.
Note: Article II, section 1, of the Constitution was affected by the 25th amendment.

Section 1.

In case of the removal of the President from office or of his death or resignation, the Vice President shall become President.

Section 2.

Whenever there is a vacancy in the office of the Vice

President, the President shall nominate a Vice President who shall take office upon confirmation by a majority vote of both Houses of Congress.

Section 3.

Whenever the President transmits to the President pro tempore of the Senate and the Speaker of the House of Representatives his written declaration that he is unable to discharge the powers and duties of his office, and until he transmits to them a written declaration to the contrary, such powers and duties shall be discharged by the Vice President as Acting President.

Section 4.

Whenever the Vice President and a majority of either the principal officers of the executive departments or of such other body as Congress may by law provide, transmit to the President pro tempore of the Senate and the Speaker of the House of Representatives their written declaration that the President is unable to discharge the powers and duties of his office, the Vice President shall immediately assume the powers and duties of the office as Acting President.

Thereafter, when the President transmits to the President pro tempore of the Senate and the Speaker of the House of Representatives his written declaration that no inability exists, he shall resume the powers and duties of his office unless the Vice President and a majority of either the principal officers of the executive department or of such other body as Congress may by law provide, transmit within four days to the President pro tempore of the Senate and the Speaker of the House of Representatives their written declaration that the President is unable to discharge the powers and duties of his office. Thereupon

Congress shall decide the issue, assembling within forty-eight hours for that purpose if not in session. If the Congress, within twenty-one days after receipt of the latter written declaration, or, if Congress is not in session, within twenty-one days after Congress is required to assemble, determines by two-thirds vote of both Houses that the President is unable to discharge the powers and duties of his office, the Vice President shall continue to discharge the same as Acting President; otherwise, the President shall resume the powers and duties of his office.

Amendment XXVI

Passed by Congress March 23, 1971. Ratified July 1, 1971.
Note: Amendment 14, section 2, of the Constitution was modified by section 1 of the 26th amendment.

Section 1.

The right of citizens of the United States, who are eighteen years of age or older, to vote shall not be denied or abridged by the United States or by any State on account of age.

Section 2.

The Congress shall have power to enforce this article by appropriate legislation.

Amendment XXVII

Originally proposed Sept. 25, 1789. Ratified May 7, 1992.

No law, varying the compensation for the services of the Senators and Representatives, shall take effect, until an election of Representatives shall have intervened.

Select Bibliography

Abdul-Jabbar, Kareem. *Writings on the Wall*. New York: Liberty Street, 2016.

Anderson, Carol. *White Rage*. New York: Bloomsbury USA, 2017.

Arnn, Larry. *The Founders' Key*. Nashville: Thomas Nelson, 2012.

Brooks, Arthur. *The Road to Freedom*. New York: Basic Books, 2012.

Foner, Eric. *The Second Founding*. New York: W.W. Norton & Company, 2019.

Gehl, Katherine, Michael Porter. *The Politics Industry*. Boston: Harvard Business Review Press, 2020.

Gorsuch, Neil. *A Republic, If You Can Keep It*. New York: Crown Forum, 2019.

Hillsdale College Politics Department, ed. *The U.S. Constitution: A Reader*. Hillsdale: Hillsdale College Press, 2012.

Lepore, Jill. *These Truths*. New York: W.W. Norton & Company, 2018.

Levin, Yuval. *The Great Debate*. New York: Basic Books, 2014.

Mettler, Suzanne, Robert Lieberman. *Four Threats*. New York: St. Martin's Press, 2020

Orman, Greg. *A Declaration of Independents*. Austin: Greenleaf Book Group Press, 2016.

Shyamalan, M. Night. *I Got Schooled*. New York: Simon & Schuster, 2013.

Sowell, Thomas. *Discrimination and Disparities*. New York: Basic Books, 2019.

Sowell, Thomas. *Wealth, Poverty and Politics*. New York: Basic Books, 2015.

Walker, David. *America In 2040: Still A Superpower?*. Bloomington: AuthorHouse, 2020.

Will, George. *The Conservative Sensibility*. New York: Hachette Books, 2019.

Notes

Introduction

1. David M. Walker, *America in 2040: Still a Superpower?* (Bloomington: AuthorHouse, 2020), 251

2. Jill Lepore, *These Truths* (New York: W.W. Norton & Company, 2018), 783

3. Nitin Nohria, *Talks at GS* (YouTube, September 29, 2017)

4. Kareem Abdul-Jabbar, *Writings on the Wall* (New York: Liberty Street, 2016), 4

Chapter 1: Our Founding

1. George F. Will, *The Conservative Sensibility* (New York: Hachette Books, 2019), 473

2. Paul Meany, "Cicero's Natural Law and Political Philosophy," *Libertarianism.org*, August 31, 2018,

3. https://libertarianism.org/columns/ciceros-natural-law-political-philosophy, 7-8

4. Lepore, *These Truths*, 54-55

5. Larry P. Arnn, *The Founders' Key* (Nashville: Thomas Nelson, 2012), 48

6. *Encyclopedia Britannica*, https://britannica.com/topic/democracy (January 28, 2020), 22

7. Arnn, *The Founders' Key,* 59

8. "Natural Rights," *Constitutional Rights Foundation*, 2020, 2

9. *Encyclopedia Britannica*, https://britannica.com/topic/democracy (January 28, 2020), 22

10. Will, *The Conservative Sensibility*, 8

11. Arnn, *The Founders' Key*, 87

12. Ibid., 11

13. Ibid., 19

14. Abdul-Jabbar, *Writings on the Wall*, 10-11

15. Ibid., 11-12

16. Arnn, *The Founders' Key*, 71

17. "The Northwest Ordinance," July 13,1787, *The U.S. Constitution: A Reader* (Hillsdale: Hillsdale

18. College Press, 2012), 127

19. Alexander Stephens, "Cornerstone Speech," March 21,1861, *The U.S. Constitution: A Reader*, 577

20. Abraham Lincoln, "Speech On The Dred Scott Decision," June 26,1857, *The U.S. Constitution: A*

21. *Reader*, 508

22. Will, *The Conservative Sensibility*, 13

23. Ibid., 13

Chapter 2: Racism

1. Faith Karimi, "What Critical Race Theory Is – And Isn't," *CNN.com*, May 10, 2021, https://www.cnn.com/2020/10/01/us/critical-race-theory-explainer-trnd/index.html, 1-3

2. Christopher F. Rufo, "What Critical Race Theory is Really About," *nypost.com*, May 6, 2021, https://nypost.com/2021/05/06/what-critical-race-theory-is-really-about/, 3-4

3. Peter J. Wallison, "Critical Race Theory: The Enemy of Reason, Evidence, and Open Debate," April 26, 2021, https://www.nationalreview.com/2021/04/critical-race-theory-the-enemy-of-reason-evidence-and-open-debate/, 2

4. Lepore, *These Truths*, 314

5. Eric Foner, *The Second Founding* (New York: W.W. Norton & Company, 2019), xxviii

6. Carol Anderson, *White Rage* (New York: Bloomsbury USA, 2017), 15-16

7. Foner, *The Second Founding*, 48

8. Ibid., 48

9. Anderson, *White Rage*, 21

10. Ibid., 21

11. Foner, *The Second Founding*, 103

12. Roger Taney, "Dred Scott v. Sandford," March 6, 1857, *The U.S. Constitution: A Reader*, 485

13. Neil Gorsuch, *A Republic, If You Can Keep It* (New York: Crown Forum, 2019), 115-116

14. Foner, *The Second Founding*, 131-132

15. Ibid., 132-133

16. Anderson, *White* Rage, 33-34

17. Ibid., 34

18. Lepore, *These Truths*, 358-359

19. Gorsuch, *A Republic, If You Can Keep It*, 24

20. The President's Advisory 1776 Commission, "The 1776 Report," January 2021, 12

21. Lepore, *These Truths*, 357

22. Ibid., 371

23. Anderson, *White Rage*, 49

24. Thomas Sowell, *Discrimination and Disparities* (New York: Basic Books, 2019), 62

25. Ibid., 62

26. Ibid., 63

27. Anderson, *White Rage*, 56

28. Ibid., 57-66

29. Lepore, *These Truths*, 577

30. Ibid., 577-578

31. Ibid., 578

32. Anderson, *White Rage*, 75

33. Lepore, *These Truths*, 584

34. Anderson, *White Rage*, 95-96

35. "The new ideology of race," *The Economist*, July 11-17, 2020, 7-8

36. "Race in America," *The Economist*, July 11-17, 2020, 15

37. Earlbeck Gases & Technologies, "What Is The Job Outlook for Welders?" March 29, 2016, https://www.earlbeck.com/welding-blog/what-is-the-job-outlook-for-welders#:~:text=The%20welding%20industry%20will%20face,welders%20in%20the%20work%20force.

38. Loolwa Khazzoom, "Calling it 'anti-Semitism' is itself a form of racism," *J. The Jewish News of Northern California*,

January 7, 2020, https://www.jweekly.com/2020/01/07/
calling-it-anti-semitism-is-itself-a-form-of-racism/

Chapter 3: Living Up to Our Constitution

1. Gorsuch, *A Republic, If You Can Keep It,* 117
2. Ibid., 111
3. Will, *The Conservative Sensibility,* 177
4. Gorsuch, *A Republic, If You Can Keep It,* 123
5. Ibid., 126
6. Ibid., 190

Chapter 4: Democracy: Attributes and Threats Against

1. Suzanne Mettler and Robert Lieberman, *Four Threats* (New York: St. Martin's Press, 2020), 11-12
2. Ibid., 14
3. Ibid., 19
4. Ibid., 25

Chapter 5: Congress's Dereliction of Duty

1. Gorsuch, *A Republic, If You Can Keep It,* 40
2. "Executive Order," *History.com,* August 21, 2018, https://www.history.com/topics/us-government/executive-order, 1
3. Will, *The Conservative Sensibility,* 135-136
4. Michael Rappaport, "A Stronger Separation of Powers for Administrative Agencies," *The Regulatory*
5. *Review,* December 18, 2019, https://www.theregreview.org/2019/12/18/rapport-stronger-separation-
6. powers-administrative-agencies/, 2
7. Will, *The Conservative Sensibility,* 124
8. Arnn, *The Founders' Key,* 18
9. Will, *The Conservative Sensibility,* 127
10. Ibid., 127
11. Gorsuch, *A Republic, If You Can Keep It,* 66
12. Ibid., 66

13. Rappaport, "A Stronger Separation of Powers for Administrative Agencies," 2
14. Ibid., 3-4

Chapter 6: The Need for Liberal Thinking

1. "A Manifesto," *The Economist*, September 15, 2018, 13
2. Yuval Levin, *The Great Debate* (New York: Basic Books, 2014), 225-226
3. Ibid., 227
4. Ibid., xii
5. Ronald Pestritto, *The U.S. Constitution: A Reader*, 617-618
6. Ibid., 617
7. Woodrow Wilson, "What is Progress?" 1913, *The U.S. Constitution: A Reader*, 635
8. Lepore, *These Truths*, 373
9. Frank Goodnow, "The American Conception of Liberty," 1916, *The U.S. Constitution: A Reader*, 631
10. Ibid., 633-634
11. John Dewey, "Liberalism and Social Action," 1935, *The U.S. Constitution: A Reader*, 627-628
12. Will, *The Conservative Sensibility*, 48
13. Ibid., 49

Chapter 7: Getting the Right People in Washington

1. Tim Lau, "Citizens United Explained," *Brennan Center for Justice*, December 12, 2019, https://www.brennancenter.org/our-work/research-reports/citizens-united-explained, 2
2. Wendy Weiser, Daniel I. Weiner, and Dominique Erney, "The Case for H.R. 1," Brennan Center for Justice, April 10, 2020, https://www.brennancenter.org/our-work/policy-solutions/case-hr1, 7
3. Ibid., 8
4. Greg Orman, *A Declaration of Independents* (Austin: Greenleaf Book Group Press, 2016), 87
5. Walker, *America in 2040: Still a Superpower?*, 228
6. Ballotpedia, https://ballotpedia.org/Redistricting

7. Katherine M. Gehl and Michael E. Porter, *The Politics Industry* (Boston: Harvard Business Review Press, 2020), 5,121-122

8. Ballotpedia, https://ballotpedia.org/ranked-choice_voting_(RCV), 9

9. Gehl and Porter, *The Politics Industry*, 131

10. Orman, *A Declaration of Independents*, 253

11. Gehl and Porter, *The Politics Industry*, 54

12. Ibid., 56

Chapter 8: A Deeper Look into Discrimination

1. Sowell, *Discrimination and Disparities*, 30-33

2. Ibid., 32-33

3. Ibid., 35

Chapter 9: Improving Schools

1. M. Night Shyamalan, *I Got Schooled* (New York: Simon & Schuster, 2013), 79-103

2. Ibid., 107-133

3. Ibid., 158-164

4. Ibid., 164-182, 234

5. Ibid., 200-207

6. "Race in America," *The Economist*, July 11-17, 2020, 16

7. Sowell, *Discrimination and Disparities*, 169

Chapter 10: Income and Wealth Inequality

1. Arthur C. Brooks, *The Road to Freedom* (New York: Basic Books, 2012), 6

2. Ibid., 9

3. Sowell, *Discrimination and Disparities*, 1-9

4. Ibid., 4

5. Thomas Sowell, *Wealth, Poverty and Politics* (New York: Basic Books, 2015), 235

6. Ibid., 168

7. Ibid., 177-190

Chapter 11: America's Unsustainable Fiscal Path

1. Walker, *America in 2040: Still a Superpower?*, 29
2. Ibid., xi, ix
3. Ibid., x
4. Ibid., 111,108,252,167
5. Ibid., 111
6. Ibid., 251
7. Ibid., 154-155, 165-166

Conclusion

1. Anderson, *White Rage*, 176

Letter from a Birmingham Jail

1. Africa.upenn.edu/Articles_Gen/Letter_Birmingham.html

Acknowledgments

Thank you to all the authors of the dozens of books I have read over the past ten years. You have inspired me to think more deeply about society and what needs to be done to repair our divided nation. This country would be a better place if everyone read your books.

Thank you to my history and English teachers and professors throughout my life. You had more of an influence on me than you can imagine. I hope this book and my first book have made you proud, and that you realize what an important role you had during your careers.

Thank you to David Aretha, my editor, Jerry Dorris, my book designer, and Martha Bullen, my publishing consultant, who helped me bring this important message to the public.

Thank you to my family and friends who are not afraid of civil debate. I have learned much from you over the years. A special thank you to my parents for their love and for teaching me to never judge someone by the color of their skin, religion, sexual orientation, or political beliefs. The teaching has served me well, and I have friends from all walks of life.

Most importantly, thank you, Stephanie Ellison. You are the love of my life, beautiful inside and out, smart, funny, and a great mother to our son. I am so lucky to be walking through life with you. Thank you for believing in me and my desire to make a positive impact on the world in which we live.

About the Author

Davidd A. Ellison is an avid reader of books about history, politics, the division within our country, and the Constitution. His first book, *Politics Beyond Left and Right: A Guide for Creating a More Unified Nation*, was published in 2017. He received his B.S. from Bryant University, and is a Certified Financial Planner but no longer practices. David previously worked as the editor and publisher of *The Financial Corner*, a monthly financial newsletter. He currently lives in Milford, Connecticut, and is a partner with his wife, Stephanie, in the Ellison Homes Team, a real estate brokerage firm. Learn more about David and his new book, *Repairing Our Divided Nation*, at www.RepairingOurDividedNation.com.

Made in United States
North Haven, CT
01 March 2022

16657904R00117